Improve Your
BIDDING JUDGMENT

NEIL KIMELMAN

Master Point Press
331 Douglas Ave.
Toronto, Ontario, Canada
M5M 1H2
(416) 781-0351
Website: http://www.masterpointpress.com
Email: info@masterpointpress.com

Library and Archives Canada Cataloguing in Publication

Kimelman, Neil
    Improve your bidding judgment / written by Neil Kimelman.

ISBN 978-1-897106-29-7

1. Contract bridge–Bidding. I. Title.

GV1282.4.K52 2008   795.41'52   C2008-902054-5

We acknowledge the financial support of the Government of Canada through the Book Publishing Industry Development Program (BPIDP) for our publishing activities.

Editor	Ray Lee
Interior format and copy editing	Sarah Howden
Cover and interior design	Olena S. Sullivan/New Mediatrix
Cover photo	Olena Sullivan

Printed in Canada

1 2 3 4 5 6 7   12 11 10 09 08

Table of Contents

Acknowledgments   v
Author's Introduction OR *I Tried My Best*   ix

Chapter 1: Partnership 101 OR *Singing in the Same Key*   1
    You light up my life   3
    Philosophy 101   3
    Keys to constructive bidding   6

Chapter 2: Softly, Softly OR *The Art of Slam Investigation*   11
    More traffic lights   14
    Shortness-showing bids   18

Chapter 3: High-Level Decisions OR *It's Lonely at the Top—
and Scary!*   23
    The Law of Total Tricks   26
    Forcing pass auctions   28

Chapter 4: The 'Double or Bid On' Decision OR *How Many Sides
Does This Coin Have?*   35
    Low-level 'double or bid on' decisions   40

Chapter 5: Overcall or Takeout Double? OR *The Frying Pan or
the Fire?*   43
    Overcalling 101   45
    The overcall versus the takeout double   47

Chapter 6: Notrump Openings OR *Victims of Abuse*   55
    Real 1NT openings—and exceptions   58
    2NT openings   59
    The myth of the missed game   61
    Interference   61
    More on the five-card major   62
    When all is said and done...   64

Chapter 7: Bidding in Competition OR *Surviving the
Post-Mortem*   65
    Get in early, the higher the better   67
    Have good quality suits for your overcalls   67
    With a good hand in a competitive auction, show
    distribution first, then value   68
    If you know what to bid, bid it   70
    It is okay not to be perfect   72

Chapter 7 continued...

Keep an open mind as the auction proceeds 73
Strategic bidding (or thinking ahead) 74
Fit-showing bids 77
The late double 78
Predicting the auction 79

Chapter 8: Unusual Situations OR *Nobody Told Me There'd Be Days Like This* 81
Bidding for a lead 86
Asking for keycards in secondary suit 87
Responding 1♠ to 1♡ 87
Bidding again after preempting 88
Jockeying the opponents into an inferior contract 88

Chapter 9: Threenotrumpmania OR *Nine Tricks Are Easier Than Ten* 91
The opponents' bidding 93
Soft stuff 93
Stretcccchhhhhing 93

Chapter 10: Balancing OR *Boldly Going Where No Human Has Gone Before* 97
Degree of fit found by the opponents 99
Matchpoints or teams scoring 99
Balancing against 1NT 100

Chapter 11: Getting Out While the Getting Is Good OR *Misfits* 103

Chapter 12: Accepting Invitation OR *Am I Declarer?* 109
Issues to consider when deciding whether to accept a game invitation 111
Inviting games—NOT! 116

Chapter 13: Now It's Your Turn OR *Did I Waste My Money on This Book?* 123
Problems 125
Solutions 145

ACKNOWLEDGMENTS

To my parents Edwin and Zelma, who taught me to play bridge when I was nine years old; my daughter Erin for her suggestions on the title for this book; my son Kyle for his support.

I would also like to acknowledge my long-time partner (1976–2004) Bob Kuz, who is very familiar with some of these hands.

To my good friend and sometime partner, Bob Todd, who served as a devil's advocate and critiqued the content. To Karl Gohl, my current partner, who taught me some really great conventions and treatments.

Finally, to my wife Colleen. Our partnership has lasted longer than any of my bridge ones. Thank you all.

Neil Kimelman
June, 2008

Author's Introduction -or-
I Tried My Best

The real secret of the expert
is to make logic seem
like flair.

– Hugh Kelsey

Bidding is where you win and lose at bridge. Sure, defense is important, but often their contract is going to come home no matter what you do. If you want to improve your defense, read a Woolsey or Kelsey book. Superior declarer play can also help you win, but once again, read Watson's *Play of the Hand*. Add in Clyde Love's *Bridge Squeezes Complete* and Mollo's *Bridge in the Menagerie* for technique and imagination, respectively, and you have a solid declarer play foundation.

Bidding is where it's at! It is where the majority of IMPs and matchpoints are won and lost. It's great to have a well-honed bidding system, with well-discussed conventions and treatments. When they come up, they can greatly reduce areas of uncertainty and allow us to make better bidding decisions. But those pesky opponents! They are always bidding, especially when we don't want them to bid. Plus, they jump levels, and take away our bidding space. To make matters worse, their bids show something completely artificial, totally unrelated to the suit they bid. Unfortunately, our own conventions are often rendered useless in these ambiguous situations.

I suggest two additional tools are needed to supplement your specific agreements:

1) A partnership philosophy.
I played with the same partner for twenty-eight years, from 1976 to 2004. Unfortunately, we did not always get out and play as often as we would have liked to, due to the other priorities in our lives. However, this didn't stop us from being very effective when we did play. The reason is that we had general principles that guided us in unfamiliar auctions and situations.

2) Good judgment.
This book is all about the thinking that is needed to make good bidding decisions, which will also make life easier for your partner.

How to get the most out of this book
The scoring is usually teams (IMPs), but sometimes the deals come from pairs (matchpoints). Although all can benefit from the book, most of the problems are intended for intermediate and advanced players. Some of the key points have been included as Tips that you can find highlighted throughout the book.

Although I have tried to stay away from recommending systems and conventions, you will see a bias to 2/1 game forcing. I have also included some discussion of shortness-showing bids and other methods that I feel are important in enhancing your bidding judgment.

I have used 99% real hands. For that reason I have usually included names of the participants and the full deal. Among the top-level players you will find involved are the following:

Balcombe, Bates, Bramley, Cohen, Daigneault, De Falco, El Ahmady, Fallenius, Fantoni, Forrester, Fredin, Garner, Gartaganis, Gitelman, Graves, Greco, Grue, Hamilton, Hamman, Hampson, Helgemo, Helness, Kantar, Kokish, Lasut, Lauria, Lazard, Lindkvist, Madala, Mahaffey, Maksymetz, Manfield, Manoppo, Meckstroth, Mittelman, Morse, Moss, Muller, Nunes, Passell, Pavlicek, Rodwell, Rosenkranz, Sadek, Sanborn, Silver, Smith, Smolen, Sokolow, Soloway, Todd, Versace, Weinstein, Welland, Wolff, Zia.

Approximately half the material is from personal knowledge and experience, although there are quite a few deals taken from recent World and North American Bridge Championships (NABC) events. Two of the major events from which material is drawn are the annual Canadian National Team Championships (CNTC) and the Canadian Open Pairs Championships (COPC).

Finally, I have tried to inject humor into my writing. This, I hope, will serve two purposes: make the reading and learning more fun, and help us remember that even though it is our passion, bridge is just a game where we can fiercely compete, while still enjoying the company of those around us.

I sincerely hope you will find this book valuable as you aspire to improve your overall bridge performance and enjoyment at the table.

Neil Kimelman

Chapter 1

PARTNERSHIP 101 -OR-
SINGING IN THE SAME KEY

*"Where's the hand you held
during the auction?"*

- A comment Jan Janitschke sometimes made
when dummy came down.

You light up my life

To aid our discussion, I will use the analogy of traffic lights to help in decisions. I encourage their use when at the table or in discussions with partner. Essentially:

GREEN LIGHT

I have a maximum for my bidding

or

I have no wasted values

or

The bidding has made my hand better

YELLOW LIGHT

I have some wasted values

or

Not sure if we have a good enough fit for this level

or

I have defensive values

RED LIGHT

We are off two aces for a small slam
(or one ace for a grand slam)

or

I want to penalize our opponents

or

I don't have what I said I did

Traffic light terminology is something that almost everyone can visualize and understand, which is why I find it very effective.

Philosophy 101

You can't make informed decisions in the bidding unless you know what partner's (and the opponents') bids mean. If there is no consistency then it becomes more of a random contest. However, skilled players want to take advantage of their skill. They also want to take advantage of their better judgment, methods and temperament—all attributes that are worth seeking.

> **Tip 1** Have your bid—be disciplined.

If you always do that, partner will make better decisions and you will build partnership confidence.

> **Tip 2** Show partner what you've got.

Yes, this will help the opponents sometimes, but in the long run it will better serve you and your partner.

These first two Tips are cornerstones for an effective partnership. The more consistent you can be, the better chance your partner can make the right choices. The opposite is obviously also true. *Discipline, discipline, discipline.* You will see that all through the book I will say, 'You have shown your hand, trust partner'. Your partnership will not be able to do this unless you follow Tips 1 and 2.

> **Tip 3** Have discussions with partner.

One of the fascinations of bridge is that we are always encountering new situations. It is good practice to keep discussing what you think certain bids would mean in these instances. The key is to ensure that you and your partner are on the same wavelength. The following are examples of *some* of the questions that I feel all partnerships need to ask themselves:

a) Opening bids
Light or solid? What about in third seat?

b) Weak two-bids
What do they promise at various vulnerabilities? What about in first or second seat, vulnerable against not?

c) Preempts

What do they show? How does this change depending on seat and vulnerability?

d) Cuebids versus pattern bids

What is the partnership preference? In this auction, for example,

WEST	NORTH	EAST	SOUTH
	pass	pass	1♠
pass	2♣	pass	3♡
pass	4♠	pass	5♢

is 5♢ a cuebid or showing your pattern, in this case short clubs?

e) Reopening doubles

Do you always protect when partner passes an overcall, in case partner wants to penalize the opponents?

f) In the auction below, how many points does the double show?

WEST	NORTH	EAST	SOUTH
1NT	pass	pass	dbl

g) In the following auction, what does the second double promise?

WEST	NORTH	EAST	SOUTH
	1♢	1♠	pass
pass	dbl	2♣	dbl

Most experts agree it shows a trap pass of spades. But is it also a penalty double of 2♣? If not, does it promise a minimum number of clubs? Again, many experts agree that doubler should have at least two clubs, but this is definitely not a universal understanding.

Here's an example that shows how having firm partnership agreements can pay off. In the 2006 CNTC qualifying round, Karl Gohl and I bid these hands as follows:

	West		East	
	Gohl		Kimelman	
	♠ K		♠ A J 7 4	
	♡ J 10 5		♡ A 7 4 3	
	◇ 10 6		◇ K 8 5 3	
	♣ A K Q J 8 5 3		♣ 4	

WEST	NORTH	EAST	SOUTH
3♣	pass	3NT	all pass

I was able to bid 3NT because we had agreed that three of a minor, in first or second seat vulnerable, would show this type of hand.

It is critical to have had these discussions with anyone that you plan to play with regularly, and to have laid down some firm agreements. That is not to say that you won't step out every once in a while, but ideally it will be when partner is not likely to be affected by your flight of fancy.

KEYS TO CONSTRUCTIVE BIDDING

Bidding is the language of bridge. It is the way we communicate (legally!) with our partner. So it is important to have clear agreements and use the language to our best advantage. My next piece of advice:

> **Tip 4** If you know where you belong—bid it!

Quite often you will be able to make a **red light** bid when partner has closely described his hand. An obvious example is bidding 3NT over 1NT. Another less obvious example is bidding 3NT in the following auction:

OPENER	RESPONDER
1♠	2♣
2◇	3NT

This would show a hand that is rich in stoppers in the unbid suit, minimum values and no interest in other contracts—intended to be a drop-dead bid. Responder's hand might look like this:

♠ 7 ♡ K J 10 8 ◇ Q J 5 ♣ K Q 10 8 7

This is an example of bidding where you think you belong. Partner may bid more, if he has an unusual hand, but that is okay as you have accurately described your holding.

The other big advantage of this approach is that it takes away bidding space, thus not giving the opponents an opportunity to describe their hands. This next example is adapted from a deal that came up in the 2005 CNTC. Vulnerable against not, at teams, you hold:

♠ 10 9 6 5   ♡ 8 5   ◊ 3   ♣ A Q J 10 9 2

Partner opens 1♠, and it goes pass on your right. What do you bid?

I would bid 4♠. Any other bid is too misleading, although I would rank 2♣ or 4◊, a splinter, pretty high. The advantage to 4♠ is that you take away bidding space and do not give the opponents additional information. The full deal:

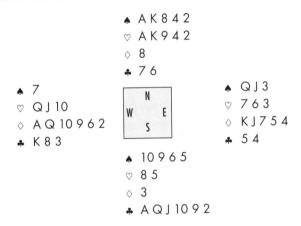

♠ A K 8 4 2
♡ A K 9 4 2
◊ 8
♣ 7 6

<table>
<tr><td>♠ 7
♡ Q J 10
◊ A Q 10 9 6 2
♣ K 8 3</td><td align="center">N
W   E
S</td><td>♠ Q J 3
♡ 7 6 3
◊ K J 7 5 4
♣ 5 4</td></tr>
</table>

♠ 10 9 6 5
♡ 8 5
◊ 3
♣ A Q J 10 9 2

Over 2♣, West will bid 2◊, and now they'll get to their good sacrifice whereas an immediate 4♠ will keep them quiet.

Tip 5 Trust partner!

This, to me, is the essence of what you want to accomplish in bidding. Describe your hand as well as you can, so that partner can make the best decision possible, then accept his decision—even if he hasn't made a bid you expected or wanted to hear. Not only will you get the best results, but also you will maintain partnership harmony and mutual trust.

Here are a couple of example deals where the players involved could have applied this philosophy:

In the 2005 World Youth Team Championships, Araszkiewicz for Poland held

♠ A Q J 10 9 5 4   ♡ A Q   ◊ 3   ♣ 9 8 7

and opened 1♠. Partner bid 2◊, he bid 2♠ and partner bid 5◊. Now what?

At the table, Araszkiewicz bid 5♠ and went down two on a club lead. Partner had his bid plus more:

♠ —   ♡ K 2   ◊ A K Q J 10 7 4 2   ♣ K 4 2

Araszkiewicz should have thought, 'Well, I have described my hand. Partner has bid game in diamonds after making a game-forcing 2/1 so he is likely to be short in spades, perhaps even void. His 5◊ is semi-invitational to slam *in diamonds*, if I have good values outside of spades. I don't, so I will pass.'

The second example occurred in the 2005 Bermuda Bowl, Egypt vs. Sweden, North-South vulnerable.

WEST	NORTH	EAST	SOUTH
Lindkvist	*El Ahmady*	*Fredin*	*Sadek*
		1♣	1◊
1♡	pass	1NT	pass
2♡	3♣	3♡	pass
pass	3NT	dbl	?

Sadek, who held

♠ 10 5   ♡ K 4 2   ◊ K Q J 8 5 2   ♣ 5 3

should have thought, 'What is partner doing?' Since El Ahmady did not bid over 1♡, he does not have diamond support. He has clubs. Clearly he could not bid them on the first round, as that would have been a cuebid in support of diamonds. So 3NT should indicate a solid club suit, saying, 'Partner, if you want to pass, great. If not, sign off in 4♣.' Instead of passing or removing to 4♣, Sadek bid 4◊, retreating to a suit that partner could not have. The full deal:

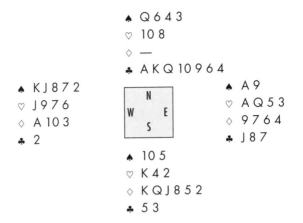

♠ Q 6 4 3
♡ 10 8
◇ —
♣ A K Q 10 9 6 4

♠ K J 8 7 2   ♠ A 9
♡ J 9 7 6   ♡ A Q 5 3
◇ A 10 3   ◇ 9 7 6 4
♣ 2   ♣ J 8 7

♠ 10 5
♡ K 4 2
◇ K Q J 8 5 2
♣ 5 3

I will close this chapter with two excellent examples of the power of natural, yet descriptive, bidding:

Sidney Lazard

♠ —
♡ A K Q 7 5 4 3
◇ A 10 5 3
♣ K 7

Bart Bramley

♠ A 10 7 5
♡ 10 6
◇ Q J
♣ A Q J 10 9

WEST	NORTH	EAST	SOUTH
Lazard		*Bramley*	
1♡	1♠	2♣	3♠
4◇	pass	4♡	pass
4♠	pass	6♣	pass
7♡	pass	7NT	all pass

This hand won the 2003 Romex Award, given annually to the best-bid bridge hand. The keys to the hand were Lazard's go-slow bids of 1♡ (instead of 2♣) and 4◇; Bramley's 4♡ bid confirming some heart support; and Bramley's 6♣ bid—accepting the slam invite and showing a good club suit in the process. This was all that Lazard needed to count thirteen tricks in hearts, and Bramley, with the ♠A, converted to notrump.

This final hand is slightly modified from one that came up in the 2005 Canadian IMP Pairs Championship.

West	East
♠ 7	♠ A Q 10 8 4
♡ Q 9 8	♡ A K 10 4 2
◊ J 9 8 5 3	◊ —
♣ K Q 10 3	♣ A 7 6

WEST	NORTH	EAST	SOUTH
		1♠	pass
1NT	pass	3♡	pass
3NT	pass	4♣	pass
5NT[1]	pass	6♡	all pass

1. Pick a slam.

Many Easts simply bid 4♡ over 3NT, and that was passed out. Unfortunately, I do not know the names of the players who had the above auction to an excellent slam.

Chapter 2

Softly, Softly -or-
The Art of Slam Investigation

*Regardless of what sadistic impulses
we may harbor, winning bridge means
helping partner avoid mistakes.*

- Frank Stewart

Slam investigation has always been a favorite part of bridge for me. There is nothing as gratifying as picking up a slam swing, or evaluating the high-level possibilities correctly when there is a lot at stake. The key quite often is to ask yourself these questions:

- What can I bid that will best describe my holding?
- What holding does partner have to make his own bid?

Here are some examples of these principles at work:

You as South hold:

♠ J 5 ♡ K J 9 8 7 5 ◊ A J 8 7 ♣ Q

The bidding proceeds:

WEST	NORTH	EAST	SOUTH
pass	1◊	pass	1♡
pass	3♣	pass	3◊
pass	3♠	pass	?

My partner, Bob Todd, found the value bid of 6◊. In evaluating other choices he decided that 4◊ would be ambiguous, 5◊ weak, and 4♡ natural. Another option might have been 5♣, a splinter. I had a relatively easy 7◊ bid. My hand was:

♠ A 6 4 ♡ A ◊ K Q 6 5 3 2 ♣ A K 9

This next hand is from 'Challenge the Champs' in the March 1983 edition of *The Bridge World*.

You, South, hold:

♠ A K 9 6 3 ♡ A 7 4 ◊ 5 ♣ A 8 6 3

The scoring is matchpoints, with East-West vulnerable. The bidding proceeds:

WEST	NORTH	EAST	SOUTH
		2♡	2♠
pass	3◊	pass	?

This should be easy. Partner has at least game invitational values. You do not have a fit, but you do have a good overcall with a heart stopper. Bid 3NT. Partner now has an easy ace-asking call, holding:

♠ 7 5 ♡ Q J 10 ◊ A K Q J 10 3 ♣ K 5

When you show three aces he can count eleven tricks, and once your ♠K is revealed the total is up to twelve. Even 7◇ is a reasonable shot after the 2♡ opener.

Some partnerships play 4◇ as a keycard ask for diamonds here, some play 4NT as ace-asking, while still others have to cuebid 4♡ to show spade support. In the latter case, whether partner bids 4♠ or cuebids, the slam would be easy to reach—the key to the hand is the informative 3NT call. Does your partnership have an agreement about asking for aces in this kind of auction?

In the competition, both Gabino Cintra and Lew Stansby cuebid 3♡, and had to guess what to do over West's 3NT bid. They both passed.

> **Tip 6** If you do not have a clear sense of the right strain (which suit, notrump) it is better simply to try to describe your own hand and hope that partner can take control.

This is definitely an art, which improves with practice. You want to keep an open mind thinking, 'Okay, what have I shown, and is this what I have? What has partner shown? Are some of partner's bids based on my calls, and if so, do I have my calls?'

The two Souths in the last example could have used this tip to their benefit.

> *I favor light opening bids. When you're my age,*
> *you're never sure the auction's going*
> *to get back to you in time.*
> - Oswald Jacoby at age 77

MORE TRAFFIC LIGHTS

I find it helpful to use the traffic lights as guides. I will say to myself, 'Partner just made a **red light** bid.' Or, 'That is a **yellow light** so I should not bid more without extras.' Or, 'Every bid partner has made has been a **green light**.'

Let's take a look at some concrete examples.

You hold as South:

♠ 10 9 7 ♡ K Q 9 6 2 ◇ A 5 4 ♣ K 5

Vulnerable versus not at IMPs, the bidding has gone:

WEST	NORTH	EAST	SOUTH
		1♣	1♡
pass	4♢¹	pass	?

1. Splinter.

Since you have a good overcall, and no apparent wasted diamond values, don't sign off in 4♡. This is a **green light** hand. Remember that partner could have just bid 4♡ if he had no slam aspirations. I would bid 5♣, although a 5♢ cuebid is possible.

If over 5♣ partner bids 5♢, showing a void, you can now bid 5♡. This is an example of a **yellow light** saying either, 'Partner your 5♢ bid has made my hand worse', or 'I have nothing else to show'. If, on the other hand, partner bids 5♡ after your 5♣ bid, this would be a **yellow light** saying, 'I have a minimum for my slam try' or 'I have no spade control'.

Partner, who held

♠ A K ♡ A J 10 7 5 4 ♢ 3 ♣ 10 9 7 3

bid 6♡, a **red light** bid saying, 'I have a spade control, but no extra values'. With

♠ A K ♡ A J 10 7 5 4 ♢ 3 ♣ A 10 9 7

partner would cuebid 5♠, which would be a **green light** saying, 'I have the ♠A, and am still interested in seven as I have extra values.'

> **Tip 7** A signoff immediately after an ace-asking bid and response is always a red light.

This is an important principle of traffic lights that is well illustrated by the next example. You (South) hold:

♠ A J 10 ♡ K ♢ K J 6 4 3 ♣ K Q J 7

The bidding at IMPs goes:

WEST	NORTH	EAST	SOUTH
			1♦
pass	2♡[1]	pass	2♠[2]
pass	2NT[3]	pass	3♦[4]
pass	4♣[5]	pass	4NT[6]
pass	5♦	pass	?

1. Balanced game-forcing raise in diamonds.
2. Shortness somewhere.
3. Where?
4. Singleton heart.
5. Keycard ask.
6. Two keycards without the ♦Q.

Pass is the correct call.

The principle that goes hand in hand with this Tip is 'Do not ask for aces or keycards if that knowledge will not help you decide how high to bid.' Instead you should cuebid, or make some other invitational call.

As South you hold:

♠ J 9 8 4 ♡ A ♦ K 10 6 5 ♣ A 5 4 3

WEST	NORTH	EAST	SOUTH
			1♣
2♦[1]	2♡	pass	2♠[2]
pass	3♦	pass	3NT
pass	4♣	pass	?

1. Weak
2. Shows unbalanced hand, usually 5-4.

Partner has shown a hand with hearts and clubs and is interested in a club slam. What do you do now? You need to evaluate your hand. On the plus side you have two aces and a diamond control. On the minus side you have a minimum with no heart fit, perhaps a wasted king of diamonds and the shortest club length possible.

Bid 5♣. This is a **yellow light** for partner, who will respect your bid and pass. My hand (opposite this) was:

♠ A 3 2 ♡ K Q 10 7 5 ♦ — ♣ J 10 9 8 7

Without this type of information from partner I would have to guess whether to bid five, six or seven clubs. If you think dreaming of seven is unreasonable, give partner:

♠ 9 8 7 6 ♡ A ◇ Q 5 4 ♣ A K 6 3 2

Here is a hand to illustrate another important principle of constructive slam bidding.

As South you hold:

♠ 9 ♡ A K ◇ A K 10 9 7 6 2 ♣ Q 6 2

The bidding has gone:

WEST	NORTH	EAST	SOUTH
			1◇
pass	1♡	pass	3◇
pass	4♣	pass	4◇
pass	5◇	pass	?

What do you bid? The 4♣ call is initially ambiguous, but it is now revealed as an advance cuebid in support of diamonds. Did you bid one more for luck?

I hope you didn't. Partner had:

♠ K ♡ 10 9 7 6 ◇ Q 8 5 4 3 ♣ A 7 3

However, don't feel bad if you did. Nick and Judy Gartaganis, one of the most successful partnerships in Canada, bid the slam (although on a different auction).

How can you tell? The reason you pass is what partner did *not* do. He did not cuebid the ♠A or the ♣K over 4◇. You might think that partner could still have one of these cards, but the reason he signed off was to put the brakes on with only moderate values.

It's important to have a clear understanding of what below-game cuebids mean in your partnership. Do they show extras? Are they always first-round controls? Here's how I like to play them, but I caution you that it is definitely not a universal treatment.

> **Tip 8** Play that a cuebid below the level of game does not necessarily show significant extra values, but it does show first-round control in the suit bid.

The only time you should not cuebid, in my view, is when you have unexpectedly substandard values for your bidding so far. Here's the converse of that: a situation where you have hitherto undisclosed extra strength. You hold in a team game as South:

♠ 7 ♡ A J 6 ◇ K J 10 5 ♣ K Q 9 4 3

The bidding has gone:

WEST	NORTH	EAST	SOUTH
			1◇
pass	1♡	pass	2♡
pass	4NT	pass	5♣
pass	5NT	pass	?

We discussed that signing off directly after a Keycard response is a **red light**, but bidding 5NT asking for kings is a **green light**, inviting you to bid a grand slam with the right hand.

What is the right hand? There are two things you should look for:

a) Undisclosed values
b) A source of tricks

Here you have both. Although you only have three hearts, you have a singleton and more than a minimum in high cards (just). But the main reason to bid seven is that you have a source of tricks in clubs. Try to visualize some hands for partner:

♠ A 6 5 ♡ K Q 10 9 5 4 ◇ A 3 ♣ A 8
♠ A 6 5 4 ♡ K Q 5 4 3 ◇ A 3 ♣ A 8
♠ A ♡ K Q 8 5 3 2 ◇ A 3 2 ♣ A 8 7
♠ A 6 ♡ K Q 10 5 ◇ A 3 2 ♣ A 8 7 6

See what I mean? In real life, partner had the first example hand.

SHORTNESS-SHOWING BIDS (ALERT: I LOVE THEM!)

Although this book is generically about bidding and not conventions, I think that a necessary arrow in your partnership quiver is the shortness-showing bid. How can you show good judgment without knowing if your values are working?

Many players play splinters in certain standard or common situations; e.g., 1♠ - 4♣ shows a singleton or void in clubs, about 10-13 HCP and at least four spades. But there are many, many other auctions in which you can use splinters effectively. Here are two:

WEST	NORTH	EAST	SOUTH
	1♠	pass	2♣[1]
pass	3♢		

1. Game-forcing.

WEST	NORTH	EAST	SOUTH
	1♠	pass	2♣
pass	2♠	pass	4♢

In the first example, North should have four clubs. In the second auction, two spades are sufficient for South if the 2♠ bid promises six of them—he might have:

♠ Q 6   ♡ A 7 6 4   ♢ 4   ♣ A J 10 7 6 5

Although this is not universally practiced by all experts, I strongly recommend that you:

Tip 9 Play that a splinter by opener in a game-forcing auction does not show extra values.

The reason is that hands with minimum values are the most frequently encountered. All you are looking for is **no duplication of values**. Here is another application:

WEST	NORTH	EAST	SOUTH
	1♠	pass	3NT[1]
pass	4♣		

1. 12-14 HCP, 4-3-3-3 distribution.

I like to play that a new suit bid at the four-level in this sequence shows shortness and invites slam providing there is no duplication of values.

Suppose opposite North's

$\spadesuit$ A Q 10 9 3 $\heartsuit$ A 8 7 5 $\diamond$ K Q 7 3 $\clubsuit$ —

you hold either of these hands:

$\spadesuit$ K J 4 $\heartsuit$ 10 4 3 $\diamond$ A 8 4 $\clubsuit$ K J 5 3

$\spadesuit$ K J 4 $\heartsuit$ K J 5 3 $\diamond$ A 8 4 $\clubsuit$ 10 5 3

Obviously you want to stop in 4$\spadesuit$ on hand number one, but bid 6$\spadesuit$ on the second one. Finding out the degree of fit is the way to do it!

Here is a hand that Karl Gohl and I bid in the 2005 CNTC zone playdowns. Our hands were:

Kimelman	Gohl
$\spadesuit$ 10 4 2	$\spadesuit$ A K 5
$\heartsuit$ —	$\heartsuit$ 10 8 4
$\diamond$ K Q 9 5 2	$\diamond$ A J 10 8
$\clubsuit$ A J 10 9 2	$\clubsuit$ Q 8 3
1$\diamond$	2$\heartsuit$[1]
2$\spadesuit$[2]	2NT[3]
3NT[4]	4$\clubsuit$[5]
4NT[6]	5$\clubsuit$[7]
5$\diamond$[8]	6$\diamond$

1. Game-forcing diamond raise, no shortness.
2. Artificial, showing shortness somewhere.
3. Asks for short suit.
4. Heart void.
5. Keycard ask.
6. Two keycards with the queen of trumps.
7. Specific king ask.
8. No kings.

I am not saying you should use our methods, but we were able to diagnose the perfect fit and pick up 12 IMPs due to the shortness-asking ability.

I will close this chapter with two more real-life examples demonstrating the power of splinters:

The first is from the 2005 Venice Cup round robin, China vs. Argentina.

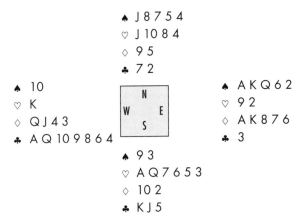

♠ J 8 7 5 4
♡ J 10 8 4
♦ 9 5
♣ 7 2

♠ 10
♡ K
♦ Q J 4 3
♣ A Q 10 9 8 6 4

♠ A K Q 6 2
♡ 9 2
♦ A K 8 7 6
♣ 3

♠ 9 3
♡ A Q 7 6 5 3
♦ 10 2
♣ K J 5

With both sides vulnerable, the bidding at one table went:

WEST	NORTH	EAST	SOUTH
Boldt	J. Wang	Iribarren	Sun
1♣	pass	1♠	2♡
3♣	pass	3♦	pass
4♦	pass	4NT	pass
5♣	pass	5♦	all pass

I suggest that Argentina's Boldt had a perfect splinter of 4♡ over the 3♦ bid! Then her partner could now confidently bid the slam after checking for keycards.

> *A fellow had made a bad bid and gone down*
> *for 1400. "I'm sorry," he said to his*
> *partner, "I had a card misplaced."*
> *Asked his partner innocently,*
> *"Only one card?"*
> - Charles Goren

Finally, as reported in the 2003 New Orleans NABC *Daily Bulletin*, Jade Barrett and Diana Marquardt bid beautifully, albeit aggressively, to a 6♡ slam with these cards:

Barrett

♠ A K J 10 4
♡ A 10 5
◇ A 3
♣ 7 5 4

```
      N
  W       E
      S
```

Marquardt

♠ 9 3
♡ K J 8 7 4 3 2
◇ K 8 7 4
♣ —

WEST	NORTH	EAST	SOUTH
	Barrett		*Marquardt*
—	1NT[1]	pass	2◇[2]
pass	2♡	pass	4♣[3]
pass	4◇[4]	pass	5♣[4]
pass	6♡[5]	all pass	

1. 14-17.
2. Transfer.
3. Splinter.
4. First-round control.
5. An established partnership might look for a grand slam, but I suspect this auction won the Barrett team 13 IMPs in their morning KO event.

Chapter 3

HIGH-LEVEL DECISIONS -OR-
IT'S LONELY AT THE TOP—AND SCARY!

*The sum of all technical
knowledge cannot make a
master contract player.*

- Ely Culbertson

The high-level auction is an area where a vast number of matchpoints and IMPs can be, and usually are, won and lost on one decision. For example, in a local team game recently my teammates chose to double 4♠ in a competitive auction. It made. At the other table our opponents bid on instead and made 6♣ doubled. That was 20 IMPs. Huge! So what are some of the secrets to high-level competitive decisions? Here are some bridge mantras and ideas that have helped me over the years.

> **Tip 10** When both sides have a large fit, and you are not sure who can make what, bid one more.

This tip would have helped our partners avoid the above 20-IMP disaster. The thinking is that even if you go down one or two it is cheap insurance against –650 or –1430. Large fits can nullify the opponents' high cards if they are in your short suits.

Here is a prime example of what happens when you don't bid one more. This deal came up in the 2003 US Team trials:

```
                  ♠ A 10 9 7
                  ♡ K 9 6
                  ◊ A K Q 8
                  ♣ 8 4
  ♠ J 8 4                          ♠ K Q 5 3 2
  ♡ A 5 2          N               ♡ —
  ◊ 9 6 5 4      W   E             ◊ —
  ♣ K 7 5          S               ♣ A Q J 10 9 6 3 2
                  ♠ 6
                  ♡ Q J 10 8 7 4 3
                  ◊ J 10 7 3 2
                  ♣ —
```

In the Closed Room the bidding went:

WEST	NORTH	EAST	SOUTH
Garner	Doub	Weinstein	Wildavsky
			3♡
pass	4♡	6♣	pass
pass	dbl	all pass	

Clearly East is bidding 6♣ as a make. Personally I think 6◊ by South is a good call. But certainly *someone* needs to bid on. At the other table:

WEST	NORTH	EAST	SOUTH
Morse	Fallenius	Wolff	Welland
			3♡
pass	4♡	5♣	pass
pass	5♡	5♠	6♡
dbl	all pass		

Here East decided to bid more slowly, hoping he and his partner could better judge what to do. It could have worked. West had a tough bid over 6♡. However, he was blinded by the ♡A, and did not consider partner's bidding, which would indicate a strong playing hand, likely at least 7-5. He knew that there was the possibility 6♡ might make and he also knew that 7♣ was likely to go down one or two, if at all—for example, if partner held:

♠ A K 10 9 2   ♡ 3   ◊ —   ♣ A J 10 9 8 4 3

On the actual layout both slams were cold, so +1090 and +1660 meant 21 big IMPs to the Welland team.

The Law of Total Tricks

The Law of Total Tricks, which Larry Cohen has written about extensively, is a rule of thumb that is closely related to this Tip. Very simply, you add together the total number of trumps in your best fit, and add that to the number in your opponents' best fit. The total is roughly equal to how many tricks are available on the hand to both sides combined. The basic idea is, if both you and the opponents each have a big fit, then both sides potentially can make a high-level contract.

For this reason I strongly endorse any bids that help you assess your fit more accurately. Good examples are those that differentiate three- and four-card length in partner's trump holding (e.g., Bergen raises or a 2NT limit raise response to partner's one-level overcall in a major). I mention these to make you aware of the possibilities, and invite you to read further on these subjects.

Tip 11 The five-level belongs to the opponents.

This is a useful *guide*. Quite often both sides can come close to making game, and so it is often right to bid one more, using the philosophy in Tip 10. It may sound as though these two ideas contradict each other, and they do to some extent. The trick is to know when to apply each. We will shortly look at some examples to see the difference.

> **Tip 12** Anticipate the need for high-level judgment early in the auction, and get partner involved in the final decision.

The best way to do this, after you have found your primary fit, is to show a second suit. Let's say you want to compete at least to the four-level: bid a new suit at the three- or four-level. Partner can then judge the total fit between the hands, and bid accordingly.

This was the last deal of the semifinal match between the Netherlands and Italy in the 2003 World Transnational Open Teams Championship, with the match sitting at 45-44 IMPs.

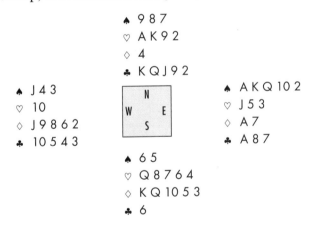

WEST	NORTH	EAST	SOUTH
de Wijs	D'Avossa	Muller	Ferraro
pass	1♣	dbl	1♡
pass	3♡	3♠	4◇
4♠	all pass		

Ferraro recognized at his second turn that it might very well go 4♠ on his left, so he showed his second suit. D'Avossa passed over 4♠, which was a **yellow light**, saying that the 4◇ bid didn't help his hand, but that he felt he couldn't double either. Ferraro, having described his two-suiter, trusted partner and passed too. In the exact same auction at the other table, Jansma bid 5♡ with the South hand. This got doubled and went down two while 4♠ was down one, for 9 IMPs to Italy, allowing them to advance to the final.

> **Tip 13** Understand and use forcing auctions to your benefit.

FORCING PASS AUCTIONS

Like the Law of Total Tricks, this subject has generated a great deal of literature. Eddie Kantar is one notable world-class player and teacher who has written extensively about forcing auctions. Simply stated, when your side has game-going strength, a pass by either partner in a competitive auction is forcing. This allows you more options with which to describe your offensive and defensive potential.

Here is a list of possible actions in a forcing pass auction example, with you and partner being North-South:

WEST	NORTH	EAST	SOUTH
	1♠	pass	2♣¹
2♡	2♠	3♡	3♠
4♡	?		

1. Game-forcing.

Since 2♣ was game-forcing, the forcing pass principle applies. The meanings of various actions by North now are as follows:

Pass—no strong opinion, often showing either short hearts (zero or one) or long hearts (three-plus). It is a **green light**, if South is interested in bidding on. However, if South then doubles, any further bid by North shows a serious slam try.

New suit—this bid is natural, usually indicating shortness in the opponents' suit, and looking for help with the decision as to what to do if the opponents bid 5♡. It denies a serious slam try, because with that hand North would pass and *then* bid his second suit.

Four spades—this bid says 'I want to play 4♠', and inferentially denies a slam try or strong distributional hand.

Double—this shows either minimum values and/or no fit in clubs, and/or a doubleton in their suit, which is the worst holding possible. This is a strong **yellow light** to partner.

This is a hand from the 1978 Vanderbilt.

Mike Passell		George Rosenkranz
♠ A K Q J 10 8 6 3		♠ 5
♡ A 8 5	N	♡ 9 7 6 4
◇ —	W E	◇ K 10 8 6 5
♣ K 4	S	♣ J 5 3

Both tables arrived at this point in the bidding.

WEST	NORTH	EAST	SOUTH
Passell		*Rosenkranz*	
			1◇
dbl	pass	1♡	2♣
4♠	5♣	?	

Passell's sequence had shown a strong hand, good enough to bid game in spades by himself. The opponents, by their bidding, were almost certainly sacrificing.

The forcing pass structure allows East, in this example, to communicate to his partner what he thinks the partnership should do, with the knowledge that he has at the time. In this case, Rosencrantz did not have a fit for spades and had length and some strength in the two suits bid by South, so should clearly have doubled.

At the table he passed, which normally would say, 'Partner I don't have any strong opinion what to do—you decide.' Passell reasonably bid five spades on that assumption, and was very disappointed with dummy. The opponents gave a trick away, but 5♠ still went down one, while 5♣ would have been down at least three, doubled!

Here is an interesting hand that exemplifies an important high-level strategy, especially at teams. It came up in the 2005 CNTC finals.

You hold as South:

♠ Q 8 ♡ A Q J 9 ♢ A K Q J 5 2 ♣ J

A twenty-count. The bidding goes, with East-West vulnerable:

WEST	NORTH	EAST	SOUTH
		1♣	dbl
pass	1♡	1♠	4♡
4♠	pass	pass	?

All of a sudden this hand has taken a downturn. Not only have the opponents not let us play in 4♡, but also I am not sure we can beat 4♠. Since they are vulnerable I decided to take insurance, along the lines of Tip 11, and bid one more. However, I bid 5♢, not 5♡. This bid tells partner that I have a longer diamond suit, and in case his hearts are poor or we have a better diamond fit, 5♢ will be safer. Was I ever right!

This was the full deal:

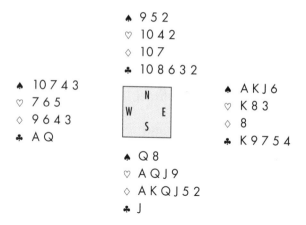

♠ 9 5 2
♡ 10 4 2
♢ 10 7
♣ 10 8 6 3 2

♠ 10 7 4 3
♡ 7 6 5
♢ 9 6 4 3
♣ A Q

♠ A K J 6
♡ K 8 3
♢ 8
♣ K 9 7 5 4

♠ Q 8
♡ A Q J 9
♢ A K Q J 5 2
♣ J

As you can see, 5♢ is down one and 5♡ is down many, while 4♠ may or may not make. However, if you exchange West's ♢3 for the ♣3, 4♠ makes easily.

One point to note is that since North had to bid on the first round, his pass of 4♠ is not forcing, but only says, 'I have nothing to say'. It suggests a bad hand, which describes North's holding nicely.

Here is another one:

♠ A 7 6 ♡ K J 10 5 ♢ K 10 3 ♣ A K 2

Being too strong for 1NT, you open 1♣ and partner bids 1♡. Looks easy... but what do you do? At the table, South bid 4♡. Partner with

♠ K Q J ♡ Q 8 7 4 2 ♢ A ♣ 7 5 4 3

trotted out Blackwood and got you to a bad slam. Is there a problem? If so, what is it?

I believe that the 4♡ bid is wrong for a couple of reasons. First, your hand is not good enough. Besides having only 18 HCP, you have no distribution. How does partner know whether you are balanced or semi-balanced?

An alternative that most experts would choose is a bid of 2NT, showing 18-19 HCP and a balanced hand. Over the likely 3NT by partner, you can pull to 4♡, confident that partner will have a good idea as to both your strength and distribution.

Another advantage of bidding 2NT with this type of hand is that when you bid 3♡ directly partner can infer that your hand is either unbalanced or semi-balanced, such as 2-4-2-5 shape.

Okay, now try this one. You are South.

♠ 5 3 ♡ 9 5 3 2 ♢ A K Q 10 9 3 ♣ 10

The bidding goes:

WEST	NORTH	EAST	SOUTH
	1♣	pass	1♢
pass	1♠	pass	2♢
pass	5♢	pass	?

This should be easy. Bid 6♢. Partner has enough values to commit to game when all you showed was a minimum response, no fit for partner, and at least six diamonds. You might hold:

♠ Q 5 ♡ K 9 3 2 ♢ K 10 9 8 6 4 ♣ 10

Also, partner has implied he is short in hearts by bidding spades and clubs, then strongly supporting diamonds.

I was shocked when the author of the article in which this hand was described suggested that North was at fault for not getting to the slam! My view is almost the exact opposite. By making a value call of 5♢, North paved the way to easily getting to six. However, South did not take into account the difference between what he promised and what he actually had, thus what partner needed. As an aside, most experts would rebid 3♢, not 2♢, over 1♠.

Sometimes you know what you want to do, but need strategy to accomplish that goal. This spectacular result is from way back. It occurred at the 1976 Nationals in Salt Lake City, which happened to be my first big tournament.

Your hand as South is:

♠ K   ♡ —   ◇ A K J 9 8 6 2   ♣ K Q J 8 5

Playing matchpoints, vulnerable against not, the bidding goes:

WEST	NORTH	EAST	SOUTH
			1◇
pass	1♠	3♡	4♣
4♡	6♣	pass	?

What do you bid? First, we need to examine the previous bidding. It looks like partner has both black aces and a second-round heart control. What else can he have? The ♡A and the ♣A? With those cards, partner might have bid 5♡ on the way to 6♣. Also, it is likely that one of your heart-bidding opponents has the ♡A.

What will happen if you bid what you think you can make—7♣? The opponents at this vulnerability will likely take the sacrifice. Is there anything you can do about this?

Mike Smolen passed! His reasoning was the opponents would be likely to sacrifice in 6♡ over 6♣, but then might not sacrifice against seven 'knowing' that the opponents were 'pushed' to the grand slam. Smolen got what he wished for. West sacrificed in 6♡ and Smolen duly pulled his partner's double to 7♣. The opponents let the logic of the auction dictate that 7♣ had a good chance to go down, since it hadn't been bid on the previous round. This created a well-earned swing as Smolen's teammates sacrificed in 7♡ after a different auction.

The full deal:

```
                    ♠ A 9 8 7
                    ♡ Q 6 5
                    ◇ Q 3
                    ♣ A 10 9 3
   ♠ Q J 10 4                        ♠ 6 5 3 2
   ♡ 10 8 3 2         N              ♡ A K J 9 7 4
   ◇ 7 5           W     E           ◇ 10 4
   ♣ 7 6 4            S              ♣ 2
                    ♠ K
                    ♡ —
                    ◇ A K J 9 8 6 2
                    ♣ K Q J 8 5
```

Here is a final high-level competitive decision for this chapter. You, East, hold at favorable vulnerability:

♠ — ♡ Q 8 3 2 ◇ A J 4 ♣ A J 7 6 5 2

Let's look at what you bid with this hand in various auctions.

WEST	NORTH	EAST	SOUTH
		1♣	1♠
2♡	3♠	?	

A bid of 4♡ seems reasonable. It would be nice to bid 4♠, but you really don't have the values for that bid.

WEST	NORTH	EAST	SOUTH
		1♣	1♠
2♡	4♠	?	

In this situation, 5♡ is comfortable. You are suggesting an offensively oriented hand with spade shortness.

WEST	NORTH	EAST	SOUTH
		1♣	1♠
2♡	5♠	?	

The air is getting more rarefied. How do you feel now about bidding on? At the 2004 CNTC finals, some Easts bid 6♡. This became the final contract, sometimes doubled, but at this level neither side could make anything. The full deal:

```
              ♠ Q 10 8 7 6 5 3
              ♡ K 5
              ◇ 10 7 3
              ♣ 8
  ♠ A                          ♠ —
  ♡ A J 10 6 4      N          ♡ Q 8 3 2
  ◇ Q 8 6 5      W     E       ◇ A J 4
  ♣ 10 4 3          S          ♣ A J 7 6 5 2
              ♠ K J 9 4 2
              ♡ 9 7
              ◇ K 9 2
              ♣ K Q 9
```

The secret on hands like this is not to let the opponents push you into actions that are not supported by your cards. In fact, this example leads us very nicely into the next chapter...

Chapter 4

The 'Double or Bid On' Decision -or- How Many Sides Does This Coin Have?

A player who can't defend accurately should try to be declarer.

- Alfred Sheinwold

Obviously, this chapter is closely related to Chapter 3, in that a lot of the decisions as to whether to bid on or double the opponents occur at a high level. Let's start with some high-level decisions and work our way down.

> **Tip 14** The amount of information available is a critical factor in your decision-making.

Quite often, one side or the other will preempt or jump levels, taking away valuable bidding space. It is much harder, perhaps impossible, to describe your hand to partner when the opponents open the bidding with 4♡ or 5♣.

For that reason you should take into account that if partner or the opponents bid in these situations they are under pressure, and may not have the ideal hand for their bid. Here are two examples of applying this Tip.

You are North, playing in the 2005 COPC Final. With both sides vulnerable, you hold:

♠ 8 ♡ K 9 8 ◇ A 10 9 5 4 2 ♣ J 6 5

The bidding has gone:

WEST	NORTH	EAST	SOUTH
Hargreaves	Kimelman	Ballantyne	Gohl
5♣	pass	pass	dbl
pass	?		

What do you do? Clearly, West is putting a lot of pressure on your partnership. You may be cold for 7◇, or going down in 5◇. At teams, I think a pass is easier. However, I passed at the table in this matchpoint situation. My thinking was that East could have anything, and West might just be gambling that we would bid too much, or play in the wrong strain. Preempts work.

> *It is not the handling of difficult hands that makes the winning player. There aren't enough of them. It is the ability to avoid messing up the easy ones.*
> – Alan Sontag

I might have been wrong, but wasn't, as the full deal was:

```
                    ♠ 8
                    ♡ K 9 8
                    ◇ A 10 9 5 4 2
                    ♣ J 6 5
  ♠ Q 7                              ♠ K J 10 3 2
  ♡ 10 4 2          ┌─────────┐      ♡ 6 5 3
  ◇ —               │   N     │      ◇ K J 8 3
  ♣ A K 10 9 8 7 3 2│ W   E   │      ♣ Q
                    │   S     │
                    └─────────┘
                    ♠ A 9 6 5 4
                    ♡ A Q J 7
                    ◇ Q 7 6
                    ♣ 4
```

I was right: 5♣ went down three for +800, while 5◇ is down one.

Now you are playing in the 2005 Bermuda Bowl. With both sides vulnerable, you hold as South:

♠ A K 7 3   ♡ Q 2   ◇ K 4 3   ♣ A K 9 6

WEST	NORTH	EAST	SOUTH
Lauria	Muller	Versace	de Wijs
		pass	1♣
1♡	dbl[1]	4♡	?

1. Exactly four spades.

The opponents may be trying to push you around, and a double may yield +200 or more, when you have no game. Another reason for doubling is that your ♡Q is likely wasted on offense. Despite this, I think the correct call is 4♠. First, your opponents are vulnerable, and are more likely to have their values and/or extra distribution, and are therefore close to making their game. Secondly, West knows quite a bit about the hand—more than you do, in fact.

> *Most bridge players*
> *prefer consistency in their*
> *partners rather than*
> *brilliance.*
> - Matthew Granovetter

The full deal:

```
                      ♠ Q 9 6 4
                      ♡ 3
                      ◇ J 10 9 8
                      ♣ Q 10 8 5
  ♠ J 8 5 2        ┌─────────┐        ♠ 10
  ♡ K J 9 8 6 4    │    N    │        ♡ A 10 7 5
  ◇ Q 7            │ W     E │        ◇ A 6 5 2
  ♣ 3             │    S    │        ♣ J 7 4 2
                   └─────────┘
                      ♠ A K 7 3
                      ♡ Q 2
                      ◇ K 4 3
                      ♣ A K 9 6
```

Actually, in real life, Muller's double over 1♡ did not promise four spades, as he and his partner were playing a strong club system. However, it is also instructional to look at Muller's subsequent decision to pull his partner's double of 4♡.

The double from de Wijs here showed about 18-20 HCP, balanced. Muller, likely taking the same inferences about the opponents as above, bid 4♠. A bid like this in this type of auction usually shows exactly four spades, and at least one other place to play. In fact, four hearts doubled would make for –790, while 4♠ might have made (but would probably have gone down with the bad spade break). The reason that I am saying 'might' is that de Wijs bid 5◇ over 4♠, I assume as a cuebid, but Muller passed, thinking that it was natural. This contract was not a success—down six. Even if 5◇ by their agreement was a cuebid, it seems to be very optimistic, especially when the opponents have taken away your bidding space.

Try this one. You are South, playing teams, with neither side vulnerable.

♠ A Q 10 7 3   ♡ 10   ◇ A J 7 6   ♣ K 10 2

WEST	NORTH	EAST	SOUTH
			1♠
pass	4♡[1]	pass	4♠
pass	pass	5♡	?

1. Splinter

What should you do?

If you pass and partner doubles, I think you have an easy pass. The key is describing your hand as accurately as possible so that partner can make the right choice.

Here is a slightly tougher situation, and one in which it is important for you and your partner to have an understanding. You (East) hold:

♠ 5 ♡ 9 8 7 5 3 ◇ K Q J 4 ♣ 9 6 4

Both sides are vulnerable and the bidding proceeds:

WEST	NORTH	EAST	SOUTH
	1♠	pass	4♠
dbl	pass	?	

Is partner's double strictly for penalty? Definitely takeout? Most players have the understanding that it shows convertible values. Great, an understanding! But what does that mean? Which of these hands does it show?

♠ A 4 2 ♡ A 6 4 ◇ A 8 7 6 ♣ K Q 8
♠ 4 2 ♡ A K 6 4 ◇ A 8 7 ♣ A K 8 7
♠ K 4 ♡ A Q 6 ◇ A 8 7 6 ♣ A 8 7 5

As you can see, it actually doesn't matter—pass is the right choice in all situations! If partner is more distributional, he can bid 4NT for takeout, perhaps with one of these holdings:

♠ 4 ♥ A Q J 6 ♦ A 8 7 6 ♣ A J 10 8
♠ — ♥ K Q 10 6 ♦ A 8 7 6 ♣ K Q J 10 8

LOW-LEVEL 'DOUBLE VERSUS BID ON' DECISIONS

'Double or bid on' decisions don't just occur at high levels, and at low levels they can be just as important in terms of your score. There are two common situations, the first of which involves decisions about doubling the opponents in 1NT. Here, the accepted wisdom is that you need at least 8 very good HCP to double a 1NT overcall after partner has opened the bidding.

A word of caution: beware of doubling 1NT with hands that are minimum when you have a misfit with partner. Quite often declarer can take advantage when the defenders have poor communication between their hands.

The second type of low-level double decision involves whether to double an overcall at the one- or two-level. The key factor here is the quality of the spot cards in the opponents' suit. If the opponents overcall partner's 1♣ opening with a preemptive 2♡ or 3♡, do not double if your suit is ♡A76532. You know that declarer will score at least five heart tricks with his ♡KQJ1098(4).

An exception to this rule is when you have a misfit for partner, the opponents are vulnerable, and they have not shown extra length. Suppose you hold as South:

♠ 4 ♡ A J ◇ A K 7 4 ♣ 10 9 8 4 3 2

The opponents are vulnerable, partner opens 1♠ and East overcalls 2◇.

You should double or, if playing negative doubles, pass and convert partner's expected reopening double.

Why is it right on this hand? First, you do not necessarily have a game. Secondly, you expect to score at least one of your small trumps by ruffing spades (or hearts). A possible layout:

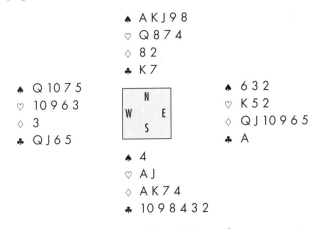

Here 2◇ is down at least two for +500, and you cannot make a game.

> **Tip 15** When you double a low-level contract you must have convertible values against other contracts.

It is very important that you can contribute to the defense if the opponents run to a different contract. In the example above, your

$\diamond$AK and $\heartsuit$AJ will be good if the opponents run to hearts. On the other hand, if you double a 2$\diamond$ contract with

♠ 5   ♡ 6 5   ◊ K Q 10 9 8 4   ♣ Q 8 6 5

your hand will contribute nothing on defense against anything else. With this type of hand, just pass and be happy they are playing in your best suit!

Chapter 5

OVERCALL OR TAKEOUT DOUBLE? -OR-
THE FRYING PAN OR THE FIRE?

*Bridge is a great comfort in your
old age. It also helps you get there
faster. One gets used to abuse. It's
waiting for it that is so trying.*

- Victor Mollo's 'Rueful Rabbit'

Overcalls and takeout doubles each have their place in defensive bidding (defensive bidding means that the other side has opened the bidding). However, there are many hands where you could choose either action, and it's not always easy to make the winning decision. You will not always be right, but the following discussion will help guide you in your decision whether to double or overcall.

OVERCALLING 101

There are three reasons to overcall:

- To suggest a lead to partner.
- To take away bidding space from the opponents.
- To buy the contract.

If your overcall will not achieve any of these, why do it? All you are doing is giving the opponents information which they can use to get to the best contract or to play the hand better. Here is an example.

You (South) hold:

♠ Q 6 4   ♡ A 7   ◇ Q 9 8 5 2   ♣ J 10 5

With neither side vulnerable at IMPs, the bidding has gone:

WEST	NORTH	EAST	SOUTH
	pass	1♣	?

What is wrong with a 1◇ bid? Well, where shall I start? If you do overcall, perhaps they get to a suit contract and partner will lead a diamond from ◇A4. Or they may play in 3NT and partner will lead a diamond instead of a spade from a hand like:

♠ K J 8 7 5 2   ♡ 6 4 2   ◇ 7 4   ♣ Q 8

Or maybe they will bid a slam which depends on locating the ◇Q. If you read about spectacularly bid or played hands, 99.999% of the time the opponents have bid giving away priceless information.

> **Tip 16** Think about what you will accomplish before entering the bidding.

Overcalls are usually made on hands in the 7-17 HCP range. If all you want to do is suggest a lead with a suit headed by the ◇AK1094, then

7 points is okay for an overcall, *as long as you can overcall at the one-level.*

For overcalls at the two-level and above, point count and suit quality requirements are significantly higher, especially suit quality. You do not want to overcall a bad suit at the two-level, regardless of your point count.

This next example is a case in point. As South, with North-South vulnerable, you hold:

♠ A Q 10   ♡ 7 6 5   ◇ Q 4   ♣ A Q 8 5 2

The bidding goes:

WEST	NORTH	EAST	SOUTH
	pass	1◇	?

Pass. This is not a good two-level overcall. Not only can you get doubled and go down several tricks, but also you have enough high cards that they may not even be able to make a game. A possible layout:

```
                    ♠ K 7 5 3 2
                    ♡ Q J 2
                    ◇ 10 9 5 3
                    ♣ 7
      ♠ 8 6                          ♠ J 9 4
      ♡ 10 9 8         N             ♡ A K 4 3
      ◇ A 8 2       W     E          ◇ K J 7 6
      ♣ K J 10 6 4      S            ♣ 9 3
                    ♠ A Q 10
                    ♡ 7 6 5
                    ◇ Q 4
                    ♣ A Q 8 5 2
```

Down three doubled on a hand where the opponents are likely to go down in 1NT! If you want to bid, double is a much better choice than 2♣, but if your spades and diamonds were reversed, pass would be the right call. And if you do pass, you still have the option of re-entering the auction later on by balancing (see Chapter 10).

Overall high-card strength is important for two-level and higher overcalls, but suit quality is more important. You should normally hold a six-card suit, with good intermediates, such as ♠AQ10984. Not following these guidelines will often result in disaster.

THE OVERCALL VERSUS THE TAKEOUT DOUBLE

Let's now look at this subject in more detail. I will outline and discuss the advantages and disadvantages of doubling and overcalling, in various situations.

ADVANTAGES OF OVERCALLING

1) Directing the lead.

This first point is extremely important. When you have

♠ 9 7 5　♡ 9 7 5　♦ A K 10 9 6　♣ 7 5

it is clear to overcall 1♣ with 1♦ for the lead. But what if your hand is:

♠ K 7 5　♡ A 7 5　♦ A K 10 9 6　♣ 7 5

The decision is not clear-cut, but most experts would lean to a double rather than an overcall. Why? This hand is worth only one bid, and you want to make the choice that has the most to gain. Telling partner that you have an opening bid and support for all the unbid suits is more important than telling him, 'Lead a diamond'.

If, for example, partner held

♠ 6 4 2　♡ K Q 9 8 6 4　♦ 4　♣ A 8 4

and heard the bidding go:

WEST	NORTH	EAST	SOUTH
1♣	1♦	3♣	?

he would pass fearing a misfit and only moderate combined values. However, in this auction

WEST	NORTH	EAST	SOUTH
1♣	dbl	3♣	?

partner would confidently bid 4♡. In fact, a well-fitting minimum take-out double could easily produce a slam:

♠ A K Q 8　♡ A 7 3 2　♦ 10 8 7 5　♣ 6

Here is a different type of problem. As South, at matchpoints with neither side vulnerable, you hold:

♠ 8 7 3 2   ♡ K   ◇ K Q J 9   ♣ K 7 6 4

WEST	NORTH	EAST	SOUTH
			pass
1♡	pass	1♠	?

Some players would have opened 1◇. In the 2004 COPC, former Blue Ribbon Pairs winner Robert Lebi chose to pass initially and then bid 2◇ over 1♠ instead of making a takeout double. His thinking was that he wanted a diamond lead, and wasn't likely either to outbid the opponents or get doubled in 2◇. The opponents bid a heart game and found it very difficult to play, as the diamond lead was the best for the defense. In addition, as declarer, I thought the diamonds were 6-1, not 4-3!

2) An overcall doesn't give the opponents information about the rest of your distribution.

This could be important for declarers when deciding to finesse a queen in a suit which you have doubled for takeout. However, my experience has shown this is the price you pay for describing your hand accurately with a double. For this reason:

Tip 17 Describe your hand accurately.

Even though the opponents will sometimes be able to use this information to their advantage, it is usually much better to do this. The benefit is that partner can make informed decisions.

3) You can sometimes rebid a second suit, clarifying your distribution.

Let's say you hold

♠ A K 8 7 5   ♡ 7   ◇ A J 10 6 5 2   ♣ A

and RHO opens 1♣. What should you bid?

Bid 1◇. You have a lot to tell partner: a good hand, six diamonds and five spades. This cannot be done with one bid over 1♣. With so much distribution, there is little danger of 1◇ being passed out.

It is to your advantage to keep the bidding low so that you can describe your hand at the lowest possible level, and partner can participate in future bidding decisions.

> **Tip 18** If you have two suits and opening points, bid your suits.

This tip has application to a popular convention—Michaels, where a cuebid of the opponent's suit at the two-level shows a two-suiter. Expert treatment is that this would normally show either a weak hand or a very strong hand. Intermediate 5-5 holdings are best described by bidding one suit and later (you hope) the other.

> **Tip 19** When you have two suits, bid the longer first.

This is a good tip to keep in mind when you have two suits that have *comparable quality*, like the last example hand:

♠ A K 8 7 5   ♡ 7   ◇ A J 10 6 5 2   ♣ A

It is my experience that it is worth sometimes getting too high to ensure that partner knows the relative length of your two suits. However, this is not a hard and fast rule. Judgment needs to be exercised sometimes. If your hand were

♠ A K Q J 7   ♡ 7   ◇ 9 8 7 6 5 2   ♣ A

I would treat it as containing a five-card diamond suit and overcall 1♠, possibly bidding diamonds later.

DISADVANTAGES OF OVERCALLING

1) The bidding might die before you can show support for other suits.

This can sometimes happen when you have a strong hand on which you decide to start with an overcall. However, the trend today is to bid on very few values, so this happens rarely. It is a risk that, in my view, is worth taking. I am a big believer in the saying: 'If I can get by this round of bidding, I will be able to describe my hand almost perfectly'. The late Al Roth, whose philosophy was much the same, used to have a catch phrase in his answers to similar bidding problems: 'Well placed if the auction continues'.

2) A big fit in another suit can be missed.

Again, this can be the outcome when you decide that your suit is so good that you just have to overcall. It happens.

3) Defensive values are undervalued or overvalued.

Partner does not know whether you have 7 or 17 HCP—again, a real drawback of overcalling with 12+ HCP and support for all suits. One of the reasons the Italians (and some others) have been very successful over the years is that they routinely make takeout doubles with most distributions, as they feel it is more important for partner to know they hold an opening bid than to have perfect shape.

4) You might get doubled and go down when there is a better fit elsewhere.

As you can see from the deal below, you can still end up in the wrong suit, although more rarely, when you start with a double. This one arose in the 2005 Bermuda Bowl, USA2 vs. England. Both sides were vulnerable.

```
                 ♠ A K Q 8 2
                 ♡ K J 9
                 ◇ 10 8 7
                 ♣ J 4
 ♠ J 10 7 6 5 4                       ♠ 9
 ♡ 5 4 3            N                 ♡ A 10 8 6 2
 ◇ Q           W         E           ◇ A K 4 2
 ♣ Q 8 7            S                 ♣ 10 5 2
                 ♠ 3
                 ♡ Q 7
                 ◇ J 9 6 5 3
                 ♣ A K 9 6 3
```

WEST	NORTH	EAST	SOUTH
Fred	Justin	Brad	Jason
Gitelman	Hackett	Moss	Hackett
			pass
pass	1♠	dbl	redbl
2♣	pass	2◇	dbl
2♠	dbl	all pass	

Down two for –500. There is another interesting point in this hand: if you are afraid of being doubled, pick the suit where if they double, and you make, it is game. Although Gitelman's 2♣ and 2♠ bids could have worked out, I think for this reason 2♡ is a better bid than the ones he actually chose.

ADVANTAGES OF DOUBLING

1) Shows high card strength.
Usually a double shows at least 12 HCP and thus defensive values. Partner is much better placed to compete with this knowledge.

2) Allows partner to double the opponents.
Again, knowing that partner has certain minimum defensive values is often key. That is why some hands are not suitable for doubling, as they do not contain the defensive values that should be promised by a double. An example of this principle is:

♠ 6 4 2 ♡ K Q 10 9 ◇ K Q J 7 5 ♣ 5

I would overcall a 1♣ opening on this hand, not double.

3) Allows partner to bid a suit confidently, knowing you will have at least three-card support.
This is very helpful when the bidding is at a higher level.

4) A new suit bid by you later shows a hand too strong for a simple overcall.
Here is a hand I held as South at the 2005 CNTC in Montreal:

♠ 4 ♡ A Q 10 8 4 ◇ K J 2 ♣ A K 10 2

The opening bid, on my right, was 1♠. I prefer to overcall when possible, especially when I have five cards in the other major. However, this time I felt I was too strong, and I doubled. The bidding continued (North-South vulnerable):

WEST	NORTH	EAST	SOUTH
		1♠	dbl
2♠	pass	pass	3♡
pass	4♡	4♠	dbl
all pass			

The full deal was:

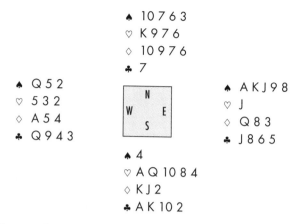

```
                    ♠ 10 7 6 3
                    ♡ K 9 7 6
                    ◇ 10 9 7 6
                    ♣ 7
  ♠ Q 5 2              N          ♠ A K J 9 8
  ♡ 5 3 2         W        E      ♡ J
  ◇ A 5 4              S          ◇ Q 8 3
  ♣ Q 9 4 3                       ♣ J 8 6 5
                    ♠ 4
                    ♡ A Q 10 8 4
                    ◇ K J 2
                    ♣ A K 10 2
```

Overcalling might have caused us to miss our cold game (i.e., partner might have had a doubleton in clubs and not raised). Four spades went down four for +800.

5) Avoids being doubled when you have a better fit.
If you overcall and get doubled, usually you just have to sit and take your medicine. It's just too dangerous to scramble around trying to find a better spot, as most of the time you just end up a level higher. Starting off with a takeout double involves partner in the decision about strain, and you have a better chance of landing somewhere safe.

DISADVANTAGES OF DOUBLING

1) Partner might miss the best lead.
This is especially important against a notrump contract, where it is usually vital to attack your longest combined suit. There is a danger that partner won't find the right lead, and sometimes that is the price you pay for doubling. However, it's hard to be perfect, and unless you have one very top-heavy suit, doubling may in fact be your best chance of getting the defense off to the right start.

2) You might misjudge your fit.
It is easy to make the wrong decision as to how high to bid, or what defensive values you have, as you may have a nine- or ten-card fit which you think is an eight- or nine-card fit.

This issue is often overlooked. For example, over a heart opening, you have a choice of bidding 2◇ or double with:

♠ Q 8 6 ♡ 9 8 ◇ A K J 10 7 ♣ J 6 4

Again, any bid can work; however, if you overcall and partner is all diamonds, he will know either to preempt or to keep quiet hoping that the opponents misgauge their fit. An example deal:

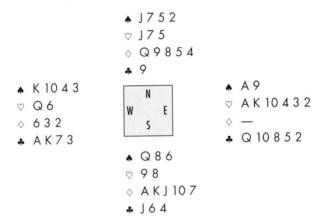

With East-West vulnerable, if South doubles East's 1♡ opening, the bidding might go:

WEST	NORTH	EAST	SOUTH
		1♡	dbl
redbl	1♠	2♣	pass
3♣	pass	5◇[1]	pass
5NT	pass	7♣	all pass

1. Exclusion Keycard Blackwood, asking partner not to count keycards in the diamond suit.

However, if you bid 2◇, things can go very differently:

WEST	NORTH	EAST	SOUTH
		1♡	2◇
dbl	6◇	?	

Probably East would pass, and West would double. Down four is +800 for East-West, instead of +2140!

Chapter 6

Notrump Openings –or–
Victims of Abuse

*If you have the slightest
touch of masochism, you'll
love this game.*

– Author unknown

I thought it was important somewhere in this book to have a chapter on preempts. Okay, so right now you are probably thinking, 'Preempts? I thought this was a notrump chapter.'

The answer is that it is both. One of my basic beliefs is that players with sound judgment will do better in the long term than lesser-skilled opposition.

At the 1979 NABC in Denver, I was a member of a team of four young Canadians (Kuz, McOrmond, Kerger) that made it to the final day of the Reisinger. We played against the best: Hamman-Wolff, Meckstroth-Rodwell, Martel-Stansby and the like. We knew we were less skilled and experienced than these players, so we hoped for wild hands, as we knew that it would increase our chances if there were less information communicated between our world-class opponents.

My point is that when you open 1NT and 2NT with a wide range of hands and hand-types, it is much harder for you (and the opponents) to judge the bidding, especially if the opponents intervene.

♠ 7 3   ♡ A K 7 3   ◇ A Q 7 3   ♣ K 7 3

is much different than

♠ 7 3   ♡ A K 7   ◇ A K Q 7 3 2   ♣ 7 3

or than

♠ 7 3   ♡ A K 7 3   ◇ A K Q 7 3   ♣ 7 3

I find myself in the opposite situation now, in that often I play against what I consider lesser-skilled/experienced pairs and teams. My mantra is: 'Describe my hand as accurately as possible, and partner will be able to make the right decision'. My thinking is that if I think I have better judgment, why do I want to 'roll the dice' with a bid that is preventing our partnership from exchanging as much information as possible?

My previous partner and I played the Romex system (devised by George Rosencrantz) for approximately twenty years. That system uses an artificial 1NT opening to describe hands in the 19-21 HCP range. So we were left with 'natural' bidding to describe all hands in the 12-18 HCP range. We were concerned about how well this would work. However, much to our delight, we found that the value in knowing partner's best/longest suit(s) on a given hand was, more often than not, a great advantage in exercising good bidding judgment.

Here is a prime example of the problem of opening 1NT on any hand that is close, irrespective of the potential drawbacks or flaws.

Partner opens 1NT. You hold:

$$\spadesuit\ 4 \quad \heartsuit\ 10\ 6\ 4\ 3 \quad \diamondsuit\ J\ 10\ 6\ 5\ 4\ 3\ 2 \quad \clubsuit\ A$$

Tough hand! Do you have a 4-4 heart fit? If so, 4$\heartsuit$ is not out of the question. There's even a chance 3NT may make if partner fits diamonds. If partner doesn't have help in hearts or diamonds, 3$\diamondsuit$ is where you want to play. Some players would cater to the first and second possibilities by using Stayman, then raising 2$\heartsuit$ to 3$\heartsuit$. Others would just sign-off in 3$\diamondsuit$. If partner has

$$\spadesuit\ 9\ 6\ 5 \quad \heartsuit\ A\ K\ Q\ 7\ 5 \quad \diamondsuit\ K\ 8 \quad \clubsuit\ K\ J\ 2$$

you make ten or eleven tricks in hearts. However, give partner

$$\spadesuit\ A\ K\ Q\ 7\ 5 \quad \heartsuit\ 9\ 6\ 5 \quad \diamondsuit\ K\ 8 \quad \clubsuit\ K\ J\ 2$$

and 3$\diamondsuit$ is where you want to play. Any interference over the 1NT would increase your problem considerably, and is discussed more fully later in this chapter.

I suggest that opening one of a major is better than choosing 1NT with either of these hands. Over 1$\heartsuit$ life is easy—partner will bid 4$\heartsuit$ over your 2$\heartsuit$ raise. Over 1$\spadesuit$ you have an excellent chance to play in the right spot. Some people can respond a weak 3$\diamondsuit$ directly over 1$\spadesuit$. If that option isn't available, you respond 1NT (probably forcing these days) and, over partner's rebid, you can bid 2$\diamondsuit$ to play. Alternatively, if partner rebids 2NT to show 18-19 HCP, a 3$\diamondsuit$ bid would show long diamonds with a minimum. Partner will pass with no fit, and bid 3NT or 4$\diamondsuit$ with a fit. Or better yet, a Wolff Relay of 3$\clubsuit$ over 2NT forces 3$\diamondsuit$, which you would pass.

REAL 1NT OPENINGS—AND EXCEPTIONS

I now play a 12-14 HCP notrump range. I believe it has a theoretical advantage over stronger notrump systems since you know whether minimum openers are balanced or unbalanced. But whatever your preferred range, I have also noticed the preemptive value a 1NT opening has on the opponents, making it difficult/risky for them to enter the auction. However, you need ask yourself the question, 'Do I want to do this? Is it in my partnership's best interest to "roll the dice"?'

I personally will not open 1NT (or 2NT) with 2-3-6-2, 2-5-4-2, or 3-5-2-3 type distributions unless I have a weak suit or I am intentionally trying to create a swing. My point is not to open hands blindly just because they meet the basic point count and distribution requirements, but first to determine whether there might be a better approach.

Every rule has exceptions; sometimes it is best to open 1NT or 2NT. Assuming 1NT and 2NT ranges of 15-17 and 21-22, respectively, the following hands are examples of the most common situations:

Weak five-card major

♠ 10 7 5 3 2 ♡ A J 7 ◇ K Q 2 ♣ K Q   Open 1NT

Your points are in your short suit(s)

♠ Q 9 7 5 2 ♡ A K ◇ J 9 7 2 ♣ A Q   Open 1NT

Your suit quality and high card strength are insufficient for a reverse

♠ K 5 ♡ A 7 ◇ K 9 8 5 ♣ A J 9 3 2   Open 1NT

Your system for minor suit auctions does not accommodate 2-2-5-4 shape

♠ K 5 ♡ A 7 ◇ A J 9 3 2 ♣ K 9 8 5   Open 1NT

(On this hand you are also potentially preempting the opponents out of a major-suit fit.)

A weak six-card suit

♠ A Q 3 ♡ A K ◇ Q 9 7 6 4 2 ♣ A Q   Open 2NT

2NT OPENINGS

In my view, the same principles apply to 2NT openings, which are perhaps even more abused in practice.

This is a 2NT bid:

Hand 1: ♠ A K 6 ♡ Q J 8 7 ◇ K 9 ♣ A Q J 6

These, in my opinion, are not, although many would disagree:

Hand 2: ♠ A Q J 8 7 ♡ J 7 ◇ K Q 8 ♣ A K 5
Hand 3: ♠ K 8 ♡ A 6 ◇ K Q J 9 8 5 ♣ A K 2
Hand 4: ♠ A J 8 4 ♡ K 4 ◇ A K ♣ K Q 10 9 4
Hand 5: ♠ Q 5 ♡ A K ◇ Q J 10 9 7 3 ♣ A K J

The reason I am against opening 2NT with these hand types is that partner will not figure out what I have, and cannot make intelligent decisions when he is expecting something closer to Hand 1.

All of these hands have, in my view, fatal flaws. Hand 2 has a five-card major, and Hands 3, 4 and 5 have inappropriate distribution. These last four hands can be shown by using different methods. With Hand 2, you can open 1♠ and rebid 3NT over any response. With Hands 3 and 5, you can open 1◇ and then jump shift into clubs. With Hand 4, you open 1♣ and jump shift or reverse into spades.

The key point is that *bridge bidding is a game of communication*. If you open 2NT with many hand types, you are more likely to play in poor contracts than had you bid naturally.

Here is a deal from the 2006 NABC held in Chicago, which illustrates my point:

```
              ♠ K 3 2
              ♡ K 7
              ◇ A 7 6 4
              ♣ 10 9 6 4
♠ Q 10 8 6                      ♠ J 7 4
♡ J 9 8 6 3 2      N            ♡ Q 10 5
◇ J 5          W     E          ◇ 10 9 8 3 2
♣ 2                S            ♣ K 3
              ♠ A 9 5
              ♡ A 4
              ◇ K Q
              ♣ A Q J 8 7 5
```

The bidding went:

WEST	NORTH	EAST	SOUTH
		pass	2NT
pass	3NT	all pass	

A cold slam missed. It could have been worse if North had held:

♠ 4 3 2 ♡ K 7 ◇ A J 6 4 ♣ 10 9 6 4

Then, if the club finesse wins, you make both 3NT and 7♣. However, if it loses, 3NT may go down on a spade lead, and 6♣ is cold.

THE MYTH OF THE MISSED GAME

Let's stop for a moment and address something. I'm sure some of you, when I suggested opening 1♠ on Hand 2, said to yourselves, 'Yes, that's all very well, but what if partner passes 1♠?' Some bridge players think that if you open at the one-level on a twenty-count and partner passes, you could miss a game. This is usually not true. Yes, if you open 1♠ on that 5-3-3-2 twenty-count, partner might have the magic 1-point hand with three or four spades and some shape that makes ten tricks a possibility. But what happens if you open 2NT and he has the same hand? *He's still going to pass!* Now you are playing 2NT, which is surely much less likely to generate a plus score than 1♠. In fact, I know some expert players who feel that if one of the opponents opens 2NT and responder passes you should double! The reasoning is that if it were close, responder would stretch. So responder has at most 1-2 HCP, and declarer will have no communication and will constantly have to lead out of his own hand.

Most of the time when players stretch to open 2NT it is because of their distribution, especially with six-card suits or 5-4 shape (just as South did in the example from Chicago). Although there are many factors that could influence your decision, I would suggest that most world-class and expert players prefer opening with one of a suit, when all other considerations are equal. The corollary is that the players who adopt this principle stretch when responding to a one of a suit opener.

INTERFERENCE

I find the question of interference by the opponents, whether we open notrump or a suit, a very interesting topic. On one hand, opposition bidding takes up bidding space, is lead-directing and can create uncertainty as to the meaning of some of your own calls. However, it also gives you a lot of information on the opponents' distribution and high card location. Earlier in this book when discussing whether to overcall, I noted that magnificently played hands all have one thing in common: the opponents have entered the auction, and given declarer a chance to go right.

The problem in dealing with interference over a notrump opening is that the opponents know what their suit(s) are. Having opened in notrump, you don't.

This hand came up in the Blue Ribbon Pairs, at the 2007 San Francisco NABC. You hold:

♠ A K 9 ♡ J 10 9 ◇ 9 8 7 6 3 2 ♣ 6

Neither side vulnerable, the bidding goes:

WEST	NORTH	EAST	SOUTH
		pass	1NT[1]
3♣	?		

1. 12-14.

A lot of players would like to bid 3◇ to play, but can't because it is forcing. If the option were available, most experts would make a negative double, and pass partner's 3♡ call.

The full deal:

```
              ♠ A K 9
              ♡ J 10 9
              ◇ 9 8 7 6 3 2
              ♣ 6
♠ Q 8 5 2        N          ♠ J 7 6 3
♡ K 6       W         E     ♡ 8 5 3
◇ 10             S          ◇ K J 4
♣ K Q J 9 5 4               ♣ A 10 2
              ♠ 10 4
              ♡ A Q 7 4 2
              ◇ A Q 5
              ♣ 8 7 3
```

By contrast, when the opening bid was 1♡, the auction usually continued:

WEST	NORTH	EAST	SOUTH
		pass	1♡
3♣	4♡	all pass	

It takes double dummy defense to beat this contract.

MORE ON THE FIVE-CARD MAJOR

Most of the views expressed in this chapter, especially as to whether to open 1NT or 2NT with a good five-card major, are probably in a minority in the expert bridge community of today. I suggest you read with an open mind. I do not state 'I am 100% right!' but this is what my experience has taught me to be the best approach. Decide which way makes the most sense to you, and continue to be open to changing methods if your original one seems to be mostly unsuccessful. The question of whether it is right to open notrump with a hand that includes a good five-card major is a standing agenda item when my teammates and I review tournament deals in the traditional evening post-mortem.

The first type of special challenge of opening 1NT with a five-card major is dealing with interference. Yes, there are many conventions and treatments that help you combat this interference. My partner and I play Transfer Lebensohl, which works well most of the time, but not always. The last example (from the Blue Ribbon Pairs) illustrates a situation where we, and most other pairs, would miss a good 4♡ contract if we opened 1NT.

Another issue that is faced when trying to decide how high to bid, in all auctions, is knowing where the tricks will come from. Sometimes you will be able to identify a 5-3 or 5-4 major-suit fit after opening 1NT, but not a two-suit fit, as you would after a suit opening. Yes, you might be able to cuebid aces and kings, but you won't be able to estimate the trick-taking potential of the suits accurately. A holding such as KJ is like gold opposite AQ876(x), very good opposite AQ76, good opposite AQ7 and may be useless opposite AQ. Look at this hand:

```
          ♠ K 9 2
          ♡ A Q 10 8 5
          ◇ 2
          ♣ K 9 7 3
              ┌─────────┐
              │    N    │
            W │         │ E
              │    S    │
              └─────────┘
          ♠ A Q J 6 3
          ♡ J 7 2
          ◇ A 3
          ♣ A 8 5
```

In the 2005 CNTC, my teammates opened 1NT and did not reach a cold 6♡ or 6♠. By contrast, a 1♠ - 2♡ start would make it easy to get to the ice-cold slam. The reason for this is that after 1♠ - 2♡; 3♡, the focus will be on controls in the side suits and honors in both your and partner's suits.

After a 2NT opening bid, you often end up running out of space to find out what you need to know.

♠ K J 7 6 3
♡ K 4
◇ A 9 5
♣ A K Q

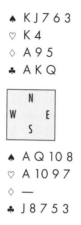

♠ A Q 10 8
♡ A 10 9 7
◇ —
♣ J 8 7 5 3

In the 2006 CNTC, my teammates opened this North hand 2NT and stopped in 6♠, with 7♠ being unbeatable. Once the spade fit was found, a splinter by South would have taken them past 4NT—no room to do everything!

A simple natural auction would be:

WEST	NORTH	EAST	SOUTH
	1♠	pass	4◇[1]
pass	4NT	pass	5♠[2]
pass	7♠	all pass	

1. Splinter.
2. Two keycards and the ♠Q.

Puppet Stayman is an effective convention to determine whether the notrump bidder has a four- or five-card major. But, as can be seen with this hand, the splinter is one level higher, and an ace-asking bid is not readily available.

WHEN ALL IS SAID AND DONE...

In summary, I believe that, in the long run, opening 1NT and 2NT with the wrong hands will have a negative effect on your bridge success.

Chapter 7

Bidding in Competition -or- Surviving the Post-Mortem

I'd like a review of the bidding, with all the original inflections.

- Author unknown

This chapter is closely related to Chapters 3 and 4. It's during competitive bidding that most events are won and lost. As in other parts of this book, there are certain key principles that are worth remembering.

GET IN EARLY, THE HIGHER THE BETTER

Bidding early allows you to compete before the opponents have an opportunity to gauge their degree of fit and combined strength. You will disrupt them more, and have a better chance of escaping undoubled.

Here's another deal from the 2005 Bermuda Bowl. Egypt was playing Italy, with both sides vulnerable.

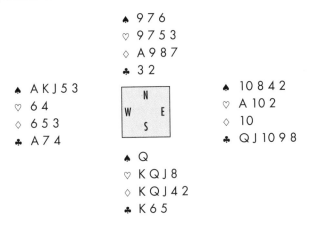

WEST	NORTH	EAST	SOUTH
Versace		*Lauria*	
1♠	pass	4♠	all pass

At the other table, East for Egypt did not bid 4♠, and Nunes-Fantoni were able to find their good 5♦ sacrifice to win 11 IMPs. As you can see, Lauria's hand is very similar to the one on page 7.

The other advantage of bidding 4♠ is that it allows you to get your bid 'off your chest'—with one bid you have said your piece, and you can leave decisions to partner from here on in.

HAVE GOOD QUALITY SUITS FOR YOUR OVERCALLS

High cards are less important than suit quality. The reason is that if you bid with a good hand and bad suit, there is more chance of your going down doubled when the trumps are stacked, and they can't make anything because of your high cards. For this reason, do not think of overcalling 2◇ over 1♡ with:

♠ K 6 5　♡ Q 9 8　◇ K J 8 5 4　♣ A 9

Pass and listen. If you had a sixth diamond, things would be different.

With a Good Hand in a Competitive Auction, Show Distribution First, Then Values

This goes back to our previous discussion of generally preferring to overcall rather than double when you have a good suit. One reason I recommend this is that a takeout double has an expected strength and distribution associated with it. Partner will make his bids based on this until he knows different. Unfortunately, this might be at a high level. The primary advantage to bidding your suit(s) first and then doubling is that you have described your distribution *and* your strength; now partner can either choose to bid, or defend by passing your double. By doubling first and bidding your suit later, you take away the choice of defending unless the opponents bid more.

As mentioned earlier, it is important to show partner where you live first, and then show your strength later. Here are two examples.

As South, you hold:

♠ K Q J 8　♡ A K Q 10 6 4　◇ Q 10 4　♣ —

With North-South vulnerable, the bidding goes:

WEST	NORTH	EAST	SOUTH
1♣	pass	pass	?

The obvious choices are double and 4♡. At the table, South doubled. The bidding continued:

WEST	NORTH	EAST	SOUTH
1♣	pass	pass	dbl
5♣	dbl	pass	?

This hand is taken from the 2005 Worldwide Bridge Contest. South at this table guessed to bid 5♡, and wasn't very happy. The full deal:

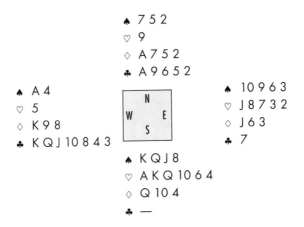

It just makes sense that partner will be able to make a better decision with additional information, which is what makes 4♡ a better call than double. And if partner held instead

♠ 7 5 2   ♡ 9 7 5 2   ◊ A   ♣ A 9 6 5 2

you probably would bid to either 5♡ or 6♡, for +680 or +1430.

This problem is similar. You hold as South:

♠ K 9 8   ♡ A Q 10   ◊ 7   ♣ A Q 10 9 8 3

WEST	NORTH	EAST	SOUTH
		1◊	?

Do something intelligent with your hand: bid 2♣. Then if the opponents compete further, a double by you would say that you have extra high card points and support for the unbid suit(s). Say the bidding continues:

WEST	NORTH	EAST	SOUTH
		1◊	2♣
3◊	pass	pass	dbl
pass	?		

Partner will bid:

4♣ with:	♠ Q 4 2 ♡ 8 7 5 3 ◊ 9 8 4 ♣ J 7 2
3♠ with:	♠ 10 7 6 5 4 2 ♡ J 7 2 ◊ 9 8 4 ♣ 3
4♠ with:	♠ A 10 7 6 5 4 ♡ J 7 2 ◊ 9 8 4 ♣ 3
Pass with:	♠ A 10 4 2 ♡ J 7 2 ◊ K 10 9 4 ♣ 3 2

IF YOU KNOW WHAT TO BID, BID IT

Quite often partner will not have the same information you have and will make a decision based on his hand, the previous bidding and *your last call*. If you are in a competitive auction, partner may bid one more where you knew it was right to defend.

We sometimes make a bid thinking that there is a safety net—we think, 'Well if partner doubles, I will pull to our suit.' There are two problems with this type of thinking:

1) Most partnerships have the understanding that bidding this way shows a stronger hand than if you had bid immediately (see the earlier discussion on forcing passes).

2) Partner may think for a while before doubling, which may prevent you from doing what you had previously intended. The huddle may potentially have given you unauthorized information that you must ignore. Your score may get adjusted if your subsequent bid could have been suggested by the hesitation. It is not relevant how clear you think it is to bid on, or what partner was actually contemplating. The fact is that you lose a lot of room to maneuver, and bidding on will often lead to the contract being rolled back to the opponents' contract doubled.

This deal came up in a recent Sectional tournament, and illustrates the effectiveness of making the simple bid.

You (South) hold:

♠ 10 8 6 5 4　♡ A 7　♢ A Q 6 2　♣ 7 5

East-West are vulnerable and the bidding goes:

WEST	NORTH	EAST	SOUTH
	3◇	pass	?

Yes, there's the possibility you have a spade fit, but the simple, effective call is 5◇. This puts a lot of pressure on the opponents. You expect that 5◇ will go down, but they will likely have a heart game.

The actual deal was:

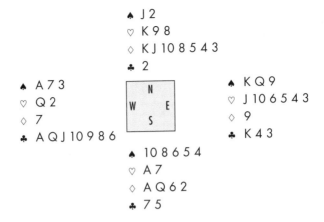

The best the opponents can do is double 5◊ for +100. Sometimes, however, they will bid 6♣, going down two.

> *Years ago there were only*
> *two acceptable excuses for not leading*
> *the suit your partner had opened:*
> *Having no cards in the suit,*
> *and sudden death.*
> - Alfred Sheinwold

Things are a little more difficult when you want to defend, but the same principle applies.

You are playing in the 2005 World Championships. Both sides are vulnerable, and you (South) hold:

♠ A 6 4   ♡ 8 7 6 5 3   ◊ K 9 5   ♣ 7 4

WEST	NORTH	EAST	SOUTH
	1♠	dbl	2♡¹
2♠	3♠	4♡	?

1. Constructive spade raise.

What would you bid?

The Chinese Taipei player passed. His partner bid 4♠, which was doubled and went one down for -200 when the full deal was:

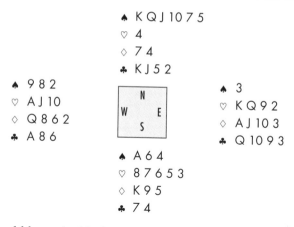

```
                    ♠ K Q J 10 7 5
                    ♡ 4
                    ◊ 7 4
                    ♣ K J 5 2
  ♠ 9 8 2                              ♠ 3
  ♡ A J 10          N                  ♡ K Q 9 2
  ◊ Q 8 6 2      W     E               ◊ A J 10 3
  ♣ A 8 6           S                  ♣ Q 10 9 3
                    ♠ A 6 4
                    ♡ 8 7 6 5 3
                    ◊ K 9 5
                    ♣ 7 4
```

South should have doubled. He wanted to defend, but expected partner to be able to read his mind!

IT IS OKAY NOT TO BE PERFECT

Sometimes our choices do not work out. We will go down, maybe doubled. Or they will make their doubled contract. The key is to make the best decision with the information that you have. Don't beat up partner *or yourself* when this happens. Chalk it up to experience and move on.

> **Tip 20** Learn from your mistakes.

Great bridge players and partnerships will look at previous hands—not to 'survive the post-mortem', but to learn from the experience so that they can make a better choice the next time they face a similar decision.

If you want to maintain a strong partnership, I think it is really important to have this mindset. The *approach* you take in discussing is key. Instead of saying, 'That bid made no sense!' it is better to say instead, 'How do you want to play that bid in the future?' Talk, but try not to be judgmental. Try to emphasize 'we' in your discussions and analysis; stay away from the 'you' word.

Keep an open mind as the auction proceeds

We all know that our hand can increase or decrease in value as the bidding develops. Sometimes the 'obvious' bid may not be the best, given what has gone before and what is likely to follow. Vulnerability also affects your assessment of the situation, as most people, including partner, will have better hands for their bidding vulnerable and take more liberties at favorable vulnerability. Something to keep in mind.

Here is an example from the 2000 Spingold. You (South) hold:

♠ J 8 6 4 3   ♡ Q 5   ◇ K 6   ♣ Q 6 3 2

With North-South vulnerable, the bidding goes:

WEST	NORTH	EAST	SOUTH
			pass
pass	1♡	dbl	?

This is a situation where there are three different choices. The first one is to bid as if the double did not occur. Here that would mean bidding 1♠. Personally, I agree with this theory, but prefer a better suit to bid 1♠ on this auction. The second choice is to make a value bid of 1NT. This by inference suggests 7-9 HCP, as with 10 or more HCP you could redouble. The third idea is to pass.

The second option makes a lot of sense to me, especially with this hand. You get your hand off your chest early in the auction. Normally you would have a doubleton heart, which you have. You have 9 HCP—again, right in the expected range.

I think there are two other strong reasons for a 1NT bid. First, what happens if it goes pass (or even 1♠ by you), 2◇ on your left, pass, pass? Most people would bid 2♡. A slight distortion, but you hope not too serious. Maybe, but partner would probably like to know how many hearts you have. What about 3◇, pass, pass? Now you might double, but have no clue if you can beat it. The second reason 1NT makes sense is that you are not planning to double the opponents even if they bid 1♠ or 2♣.

However, if you bid 1NT, there would be no story. At the table, the player with this hand passed. The bidding continued:

WEST	NORTH	EAST	SOUTH
			pass
pass	1♡	dbl	pass
1♠	2♢	pass	2♡
2♠	dbl	pass	?

What do you bid now?

First, you need to ask yourself, 'What does partner have for this bidding?' In this case he has at least five hearts and four diamonds. How many spades? Probably one at most. How many points? Better than a minimum for sure. Remember, you would have bid the same way with zero points! Remember too that your side is vulnerable. Partner clearly has not only shape but high card strength. East should have an opening bid, but West's 2♠ is more likely to indicate distribution than values.

To bid anything less than 4♡ would be cowardly. In fact, if I had the same hand minus the ♣Q I would still bid 4♡. The actual deal:

```
                    ♠ —
                    ♡ A K J 10 3 2
                    ♢ Q J 10 5
                    ♣ K J 10
  ♠ K Q 9 5 2            N           ♠ A 10 7
  ♡ 9 7 6        W           E       ♡ 8 4
  ♢ 8 7                  S           ♢ A 9 4 3 2
  ♣ 9 8 7                            ♣ A 5 4
                    ♠ J 8 6 4 3
                    ♡ Q 5
                    ♢ K 6
                    ♣ Q 6 3 2
```

STRATEGIC BIDDING (OR THINKING AHEAD)

Rather than praying partner makes the right decision in a competitive auction, you would like to offer as much assistance to him as possible. There are several ways to accomplish this.

MAKE A LEAD-DIRECTING BID

One way is to suggest a lead. As usual, an example is the best way to illustrate.

You hold as East:

♠ A K J 9   ♡ J 5 2   ◇ 10 7 6 3   ♣ 6 3

With neither side vulnerable, the bidding proceeds:

WEST	NORTH	EAST	SOUTH
			1♡
3◇	3♡	?	

Here is an opportunity to direct the defense by bidding 3♠. There are two messages you are sending:

1) 'Lead a spade if we end up defending.'
2) 'If you fit spades we should probably be bidding once more.'

As an aside, what if partner raises spades? Given that he really can't have four of them, you either pass with long spades, or return to 5◇ with shorter spades but diamond support (as here). With short spades and no diamond support, passing over 3♡ is the wisest choice in the first place.

On the actual hand the bidding continues:

WEST	NORTH	EAST	SOUTH
			1♡
3◇	3♡	3♠	4♡
pass	pass	?	

You have sent the message you wanted to. Trust partner and pass. The actual hands were:

```
                    ♠ Q 10 7 6 2
                    ♡ 10 9 6 4
                    ◇ J
                    ♣ A 10 5
  ♠ 8                              ♠ A K J 9
  ♡ 7           ┌─────────┐       ♡ J 5 2
  ◇ K Q 9 8 5 4 2│   N    │       ◇ 10 7 6 3
  ♣ 9 8 4 2    │ W     E │       ♣ 6 3
               │   S    │
               └─────────┘
                    ♠ 5 4 3
                    ♡ A K Q 8 3
                    ◇ A
                    ♣ K Q J 7
```

Declarer went down one on a spade lead, after guessing to ruff the fourth round of spades high and playing for hearts to be 2-2. Partner would likely have bid 4♠ if his club and spade holdings were reversed.

PROBE THE FIT

As previously mentioned, it is often a good strategy to enlist partner's cooperation by showing a second suit after your partnership has found a primary fit. This is one of the best ways to gauge whether to double the opponents or bid on in competitive auctions. Here are two examples, both from the 2005 World Senior Team Championships.

This deal is from Indonesia versus Denmark. Both vulnerable, you hold as South:

♠ A K 10 8 3   ♡ K 10   ◇ Q   ♣ K 10 9 6 2

The bidding goes:

WEST	NORTH	EAST	SOUTH
			1♠
2◇	2♠	3♡	?

Indonesia's Manoppo bid 4♠ now and guessed to double 5♡ at his next turn. The full deal:

```
                 ♠ Q 6 4 2
                 ♡ Q 9
                 ◇ 7 5
                 ♣ Q J 7 5 3
  ♠ J 7 5                        ♠ 9
  ♡ J 6           N              ♡ A 8 7 5 4 3 2
  ◇ A 10 9 8 6 4 2   W   E       ◇ K J 3
  ♣ A              S             ♣ 8 4
                 ♠ A K 10 8 3
                 ♡ K 10
                 ◇ Q
                 ♣ K 10 9 6 2
```

Unfortunately, 5♡ is cold, and that was –850. Had he bid 4♣, his partnership would likely have been doubled in 5♣ for –200 and would have won 12 IMPs.

The second deal comes from France versus Italy. North-South are vulnerable. As South you hold:

♠ J 3   ♡ A 8 6 4 2   ◇ A Q J 9 8   ♣ 7

WEST	NORTH	EAST	SOUTH
		pass	1♡
dbl	3♡	3♠	?

At one table, De Falco reasonably passed at this vulnerability, hoping the opponents would misjudge. He was right, as 4♠ is cold.

The full deal:

```
                    ♠ Q 4
                    ♡ Q J 5 3
                    ◇ K 6 4
                    ♣ 10 8 5 4
    ♠ A 9 7 5            N           ♠ K 10 8 6 2
    ♡ K 10 7       W         E       ♡ 9
    ◇ 5 3               S           ◇ 10 7 2
    ♣ A Q J 3                       ♣ K 9 6 2
                    ♠ J 3
                    ♡ A 8 6 4 2
                    ◇ A Q J 9 8
                    ♣ 7
```

At the other table, Lasserre for France bid 4♡ and did not know what to do over 4♠. If you are going to bid, 4◇ is much better. Partner now can decide what to do over 4♠, depending on his diamond fit.

FIT-SHOWING BIDS

This is an area of bidding theory that has grown substantially in the last few years. Below are two common applications, and one that is lesser known.

A JUMP IN A NEW SUIT BY A PASSED HAND

This shows 5-4 distribution in your own suit and partner's, with 7-11 HCP. As an example, a fit jump to 3◇ over a third-seat 1♡ opening could look like:

♠ 3   ♡ Q 10 8 7   ◇ A Q 9 8 7   ♣ 10 9 8

A JUMP IN A NEW SUIT OVER PARTNER'S OVERCALL

The exact same conditions apply.

A NEW SUIT BID BY A PASSED HAND AFTER PARTNER'S OVERCALL

This is a combination fit bid and lead-director. Here is an example I encountered:

You (South) hold with East-West vulnerable:

♠ 9 8 6   ♡ 9 5 3   ◇ A K 10 6   ♣ 9 7 4

WEST	NORTH	EAST	SOUTH
			pass
1♡	1♠	2♠	?

The right call here has to be 3◇, getting partner off to the right lead against either 4♡ or 3NT.

THE LATE DOUBLE

This is an important concept to assist you in judging auctions. The idea is to double in auctions where you know partner is marked with values, and you have shown your essential hand but have significant undisclosed defensive values. You are hoping partner can convert your double to penalties, but in any case you are comfortable, as you have accurately described your hand.

Here are two examples that will help illustrate this principle. You (West) hold:

♠ 9   ♡ 4 3   ◇ A Q J 5 3   ♣ A K J 6 2

The bidding goes:

WEST	NORTH	EAST	SOUTH
			1♠
2NT	3♠	pass	pass
?			

A great hand on which to double. You have shown both minors with your 2NT, but not this strong a defensive hand. Although not compulsory, it is also better to be 1-2 in the majors and not 2-1 when you are doubling spades. The full deal:

```
                    ♠ A 7 6 5
                    ♡ J 7
                    ◇ 8 2
                    ♣ 9 8 7 5 3
   ♠ 9                              ♠ 8 3 2
   ♡ 4 3              N             ♡ A K 10 8 6 2
   ◇ A Q J 5 3     W     E          ◇ 10 4
   ♣ A K J 6 2        S             ♣ 10 4
                    ♠ K Q J 10 4
                    ♡ Q 9 5
                    ◇ K 9 7 6
                    ♣ Q
```

Partner can either bid 4♡ for +620 or pass the double which will yield +500. At the 1987 European Championships, West passed out 3♠ and lost 11 IMPs.

The second hand is also from the same championship, and features a world-class player, England's Tony Forrester, in a more unusual application of a late double. He held as East:

♠ Q 7 4   ♡ —   ◇ 10 7 5   ♣ A J 10 9 5 4 3

The opponents were vulnerable and he was not. The bidding went:

WEST	NORTH	EAST	SOUTH
	pass	3♣	3♡
pass	pass	?	

Forrester doubled with a good not-vulnerable preempt and defensive values. His partner, Raymond Brock, happily converted the double with

♠ A J 8 6 2   ♡ K J 7 4 3   ◇ Q 9   ♣ Q

and scored +500 for a 9 IMP gain.

PREDICTING THE AUCTION

Often, you have a good indication how the bidding will go. Frequently, you will only have one chance to make a bid, so you want to make the most of the opportunity.

Sitting East, with North-South vulnerable, you hold:

♠ — ♡ A 6 ♦ A 7 5 4 3 ♣ A 10 9 8 6 2

The bidding goes:

WEST	NORTH	EAST	SOUTH
pass	1NT	?	

In a match between Forrester and Nickell during the 2006 Rosenblum Cup, both Gold and Soloway held this hand. Soloway bid 2NT for the minors while Gold chose to bid 3♣. I think it is likely you will bid only once with this hand, and 2NT describes eleven of your cards, while 3♣ describes only six of them. Justice was served as partner held

♠ K 6 2 ♡ J 7 5 2 ♦ J 10 8 2 ♣ K J

and 5♦ was bid and made by Hamman and Soloway. At the other table, 3♣ made two overtricks for a 6 IMP loss.

> **Tip 21** You will not always make the bid that would have been successful at the table.

Bridge is a game of incomplete information in which one usually tries to take the highest percentage action. But that's not always going to be the action that happens to work on the deal you are playing. The important thing to remember is that if you use sound reasoning and consider all the factors, then you will be more often right than wrong. The key point is to try and consider *all* the clues you have at your disposal. These include the vulnerability, the previous bidding, the state of the match if playing teams, and whether both pairs had adequate opportunity to communicate information. One of the key indicators that non-experts overlook is when either partner or an opponent fails to make a certain bid. There is always an inference that he does not have a hand appropriate for that bid.

Chapter 8

UNUSUAL SITUATIONS -OR-
NOBODY TOLD ME THERE'D BE DAYS LIKE THIS

*A knowledge of the mechanics will suffice to
put a player in a commanding position in the post-mortem.
To become a member of the upper crust calls for more, much
more—resilience, imagination, and occasional flashes of
inspiration: these are the hallmarks of quality.
And this transcends the realm of science.*

- Victor Mollo

This chapter is intended to address bidding situations that don't fall neatly into one of the other chapters. The key to success is keeping an open mind and not necessarily making the bid that seems automatic. Here is an easy one to start off with.

Playing in the 2005 COPC against the eventual winners, you pick up a nice hand in the East position:

♠ A Q 10 8 7 4 3 ♡ 8 4 ◇ A J ♣ A 4

The bidding proceeds with only North-South vulnerable:

WEST	NORTH	EAST	SOUTH
		1♠	2♡
pass	2NT	?	

I passed. My thinking was that South is marked with an opening bid or better, North has at least invitational values, I have 15 HCP, so what does that leave partner? It doesn't help to know that the ♠K or the ♠KJ is onside if I can't get to dummy. South bid 3NT as I had hoped, and everyone passed. The full deal:

```
                    ♠ K 9 2
                    ♡ A 10 7 5
                    ◇ 8 4 3 2
                    ♣ Q 8
    ♠ 5                          ♠ A Q 10 8 7 4 3
    ♡ 3            ┌─────────┐   ♡ 8 4
    ◇ 10 9 7 5     │    N    │   ◇ A J
    ♣ 10 9 7 6 5 3 2│  W   E │   ♣ A 4
                   │    S    │
                    └─────────┘
                    ♠ J 6
                    ♡ K Q J 9 6 2
                    ◇ K Q 6
                    ♣ K J
```

The ♠A lead, followed by the ♠Q, resulted in down two for +200 and 16½ matchpoints out of 17 for the good guys, as 4♡ is down only one. Here are two deals from the 2005 and 2006 CNTC events, respectively:

You hold:

♠ 10 9 8 7 4 ♡ K J 10 7 2 ◇ 2 ♣ 9 2

Neither side vulnerable. You hear partner open 1◇, and RHO passes. What do you think?

This is the type of hand that has a lot of potential if you have a major-suit fit. If not, and you respond, you may get too high. There are risks either way, but I believe most experts would bid with this hand. But what is the right bid?

Most players who faced this problem at the CNTC bid 1♠ with little thought and partner bid 2♣. 'Here we go,' you are thinking. Most players now passed, but there were a few 2◊ and 2♠ bidders.

Unless you have a convention like Jeff Meckstroth and Eric Rodwell use (they can respond 2♡ in the first place with 5-4 or 5-5 in the majors and 6-9 HCP), this hand is a problem. However, I believe that 1♡ is a thinking bid. You will not miss any major-suit fits, except a 5-3 spade fit. Partner will often raise to 2♡ with a 1-3-5-4 or 1-3-4-5 distribution. The added bonus to this call is that if partner still rebids 2♣, you can bid 2♡ to play on a decent five-card suit. And very occasionally partner will have 3-1-5-4 shape with 17-18 and bid 2♠ over 2♡!

Partner held

♠ — ♡ A 9 6 5 ◊ A K Q 10 5 ♣ Q 5 4 3

and 2♣ was not the best spot.

Try the other one...

I held as South:

♠ Q J 10 7 ♡ 4 ◊ A 9 7 6 2 ♣ A J 8

East-West are vulnerable:

WEST	NORTH	EAST	SOUTH
		1NT	pass
2♣	dbl	2♡	?

Partner has made a lead-directing call with a good club suit. But there is a 15-17 notrump bid on my right. On balance, 3♣ seems like a good call, and I made it.

Now the bidding continues:

WEST	NORTH	EAST	SOUTH
		1NT	pass
2♣	dbl	2♡	3♣
3♡	4♣	4♡	?

Again, keep an open mind. Partner is marked with at least five clubs, and probably six for his free bid of 4♣. He also has some values to make this bid.

Well, if he can bid four, then I can certainly bid five! My bid of 5♣ got doubled, I misguessed clubs (played RHO for ♣K10x) and only made eleven tricks for + 550! The full deal:

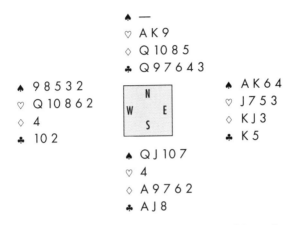

Maybe partner didn't have the greatest double of 2♣... but it worked. This deal illustrates that you must constantly adapt your thinking as the bidding and play progresses.

> **Tip 22** Keep updating your inferences as more information comes in.

It is okay to have initial ideas as to what the other hands look like, but continue to evaluate whether these hypotheses remain valid. Keep your mind 'flexible'.

Let's practice applying this tip. You hold as South:

♠ Q J 6 ♡ 9 7 5 3 ◇ K J 7 ♣ 9 8 3

The bidding proceeds:

WEST	NORTH	EAST	SOUTH
	1◇	pass	?

Bid 1♡—you have no reason to suppress a major. Nothing to think about yet. The bidding continues:

WEST	NORTH	EAST	SOUTH
	1◇	pass	1♡
pass	1♠	pass	2◇
pass	3♣	pass	?

What do you think of your hand now? You have a good hand for your bidding as there are no wasted heart values and all of your values are in partner's two suits.

What about partner—what does he have? Partner is making a game try, so must have somewhere around 16-19 HCP.

How many hearts does partner have? Zero or one.

What is the most likely playing spot for game? This is close. If partner has

♠ A K 8 7 ♡ A ◇ A Q 8 6 5 ♣ 5 4 2

then 3NT and 4♠ are good contracts. If partner is void in hearts, then 3NT will not be successful.

Do you have enough to force to game? No. However, you need to tell him that all of your cards are working. So what now?

Two bids should be on your mind: 3♠ and 4◇. Which one is better?

Surely 3♠—this bid describes your hand to a T. Partner knows you have a good hand and three spades (you didn't raise spades earlier), suggesting 4♠ as a final contract. Partner actually held

♠ A K 9 8 ♡ A ◇ A Q 9 5 4 ♣ 10 6 5

and had no problem bidding 4♠, a very good spot.

BIDDING FOR A LEAD

Here is another example of keeping an open mind, and thinking ahead as to what you want to achieve. When you have a choice of bids, usually opposite partner's takeout double, bid the suit you want led if the opponents end up declaring the hand.

You are playing in the 2004 COPC (matchpoints), East-West vulnerable. Your hand as South is:

♠ 8 4 ♡ 10 9 8 2 ◇ K J 7 ♣ 7 6 4 3

> *The average defender operates
> in a fog of uncertainty.*
> – H.W. Kelsey

The bidding goes:

WEST	NORTH	EAST	SOUTH
1♡	2NT	dbl	?

Partner's 2NT shows the minors and the double shows interest in penalizing him. What do you bid?

Bid 3◇. It looks as though at least one minor is breaking badly, and probably both. Sacrificing is not going to work well, so you should bid what you want led against their eventual contract—diamonds.

Asking for keycards in secondary suit

Every once in a while, this is the only way to find out the information that you need to make a decision. However, you must be very careful to make sure you can control the auction when using this bidding strategy.

Here's an example. You hold as South:

♠ A K ♡ A K 10 9 6 ◇ 3 ♣ K Q 8 6 2

The bidding goes:

WEST	NORTH	EAST	SOUTH
			1♡
1♠	2♣	pass	2♠
pass	3♡	pass	?

Bid 4NT. It looks like partner needs two aces plus the ♡Q for 7♣ to be a good contract, or one ace and the ♡Q for 6♣. But the only way to find out about the ♡Q is to ask for keycards in hearts! Over 5♠, you can bid 7♣ (a 4-1 heart break will sink 7♡). Over a 5♣ response showing one keycard, 5◇ would ask for the ♡Q. If partner denies it by bidding 5♡, pass!

Responding 1♠ to 1♡

Experience has taught me it is better to respond 1NT rather than 1♠ to an opening bid of 1♡ with many modest hands on which you are not going to rebid 2♠, especially when you have a long minor. The reasoning is that you cannot sign off in your minor over partner's two-level rebid, as it would be forcing.

Here's an example of this situation from the 2006 Rosenblum Cup, from the match between Forrester and Meckstroth. With neither side vulnerable, you hold as East:

♠ 10 9 8 2 ♡ 4 ◇ K J ♣ A J 9 7 3 2

The bidding proceeds:

WEST	NORTH	EAST	SOUTH
1♡	pass	1♠	2◇
pass	pass	?	

Gold, playing for Forrester, doubled to show values and passed his partner's 2♠ bid. He would have been much better placed bidding 1NT then rebidding 3♣ to show at least six clubs with decent values. Partner, I think, would have an easy 3NT call on:

♠ A 5 ♡ J 8 3 2 ◇ A 6 4 3 ♣ K Q 10

A lot better than playing 2♠!

BIDDING AGAIN AFTER PREEMPTING

This is sometimes the only way to describe a freak hand. Usually it includes two suits, with values but not enough defensive high cards to open at the one-level.

As South, your hand is:

♠ 9 ♡ K Q 10 9 5 3 2 ◇ — ♣ K J 5 4 2

With North-South vulnerable at teams, the bidding starts:

WEST	NORTH	EAST	SOUTH
			3♡
3NT	pass	pass	?

Bid 4♣. Partner should play you for this type of hand.

JOCKEYING THE OPPONENTS INTO AN INFERIOR CONTRACT

In the first example deal of this chapter, we passed to achieve this objective.

Frequently, however, you need to double the opponents in a contract that you think might make, hoping that they will run to a contract that you prefer.

Here is a deal from the 2004 CNTC on which I had the good fortune to use this strategy successfully against one of the best players and key movers in bridge today, Fred Gitelman, originally from Toronto. His partner was Vancouver's Bryan Maksymetz, originally from Winnipeg.

```
              ♠ J 7
              ♡ Q 7 3
              ◇ J 9 6
              ♣ A 9 5 3 2
 ♠ K 5 3                        ♠ A 9 8 6 4 2
 ♡ A 10 8        N              ♡ 6 5 2
 ◇ 10 2      W       E          ◇ Q 8 7 3
 ♣ J 10 8 7 6    S              ♣ —
              ♠ Q 10
              ♡ K J 9 4
              ◇ A K 5 4
              ♣ K Q 4
```

The bidding went:

WEST	NORTH	EAST	SOUTH
Kimelman	Maksymetz	Kuz	Gitelman
pass	pass	2♠	dbl
3♠	4♣	pass	4◇
pass	4♡	pass	pass
dbl	pass	pass	5♣
dbl	all pass		

We probably would have beaten 4♡ on this hand, but 5♣ was an easy down two for 300.

I will close this chapter with a very unusual situation! As South you hold:

♠ Q   ♡ A K Q 10 8 7 5 3 2   ◇ A Q 8   ♣ —

WEST	NORTH	EAST	SOUTH
1NT[1]	pass	2♡[2]	?

1. 12-14.
2. Transfer.

Wow, what a hand! However, I think there is a lesson to be learned about this type of hand. Quite often you are really interested in how partner fits your *secondary* suit. You have a pretty good idea what partner's heart support is like! What you are really interested in is his diamond holding. The best way to find out about that is to bid 3◇! This might help you judge how high to bid. This hand came from a 2006 Winnipeg Sectional. The full deal was:

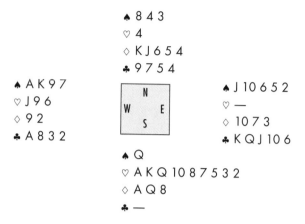

Both Souths bid hearts and guessed incorrectly what to do at the six-level. As you can see, your diamond bid would cause partner to raise you, and then you can surprise him by bidding 6♡ to make! Indeed, you might even bid 7♡ to avoid a wrong lead disaster against 6♠, hoping for a (likely) club lead that would allow 7♡ to make!

Chapter 9

THREENOTRUMPMANIA –OR–
NINE TRICKS ARE EASIER THAN TEN

*My partner is twenty years behind the times.
Nowadays you pay your money to bid; my
partner still thinks you need cards.*

– Author unknown

Man, it is hard to argue with success sometimes! So often it turns out that 3NT is the right contract. The 4-4 major fits fall prey to 5-0 breaks, and five of a minor has three top losers, but lots of tricks after that. This is especially critical at matchpoints, where the scoring can reward a good (or even a bad) 3NT. Another advantage is that most people are familiar with the common declarer techniques in notrump contracts.

But how do you know when it's right to bid 3NT? There are several indicators.

The opponents' bidding

Defensive bidding is definitely a two-edged sword, as it gives the opposition distributional clues that they can use in both the bidding and the play.

A simple example is a situation where you hold ♡QJ10; LHO has overcalled your 1♠ opener with 2♡ and partner has raised to 2♠. It is very possible that the first three tricks will be ♡A, ♡K and a third heart, ruffed by RHO. If you think you have nine fast tricks, 3NT is obviously better.

Soft stuff

The more queens and jacks, the more likely that 3NT may be better than other games. One fewer trick to take.

Stretcccchhhhhing

Sometimes we push for a good score. Again, it is easier to make nine tricks than ten. Let's look at some examples.

Playing matchpoints, and looking for a good board, I picked up:

♠ J7 ♡ A K Q 9 4 2 ◇ 7 5 ♣ 10 4 2

Partner opened a 12-14 1NT. You guessed it—I bid 3NT!

Partner held:

♠ Q 9 2 ♡ J 10 5 3 ◇ A 2 ♣ A Q J 7

Even on a diamond lead, we made eleven tricks with clubs (and the opponents) being very friendly.

Here is a hand where I did not guide the contract to 3NT, much to my dismay:

```
     ♠ J 5 3                              ♠ 10 8 2
     ♡ K J 9 8 7 4        N               ♡ A Q 2
     ◇ 4 2            W         E          ◇ A K J 8
     ♣ 10 7              S                 ♣ A J 4
```

My partner opened a weak (very weak!) 2♡ as West, and we finally came to rest in 4♡ down one. Should I have tried 3NT? Maybe. It would have been clearer were you able to open the East hand 1◇ and partner bid 2♡, a weak jump shift. In this case, you can visualize nine tricks maximum. The other advantage of opening 1◇ is you discover whether West can overcall 1♠. In this case he doesn't, which decreases the likelihood of the opponents running five spade tricks.

This next example is similar to the first one, a hand where you have a long major, but suspect there are four losers if you play in the major. During the 2005 CNTC qualifying, I held:

♠ A 10 3 ♡ A K Q 9 6 3 ◇ J 10 ♣ 10 7

I opened 1♡ and partner bid 1NT forcing. I decided to take a shot at 3NT. Partner held

♠ 7 5 ♡ 8 4 ◇ A Q 9 7 5 ♣ K J 8 4

and on the actual club lead and continuation we made ten tricks. Meanwhile, 4♡ is on a club guess after a spade lead.

Finally, here was a hand I held recently at Bill Treble's Wednesday night IMP game in Winnipeg. I held as North:

♠ A Q 9 4 2 ♡ K ◇ K J ♣ K 10 8 4 2

and the bidding went:

WEST	NORTH	EAST	SOUTH
	1♠	pass	2♡
pass	3♣	pass	3♡
pass	?		

At the table, I bid a very questionable 3NT. In my heart I knew that 4♡ was a better call, but look at the entire deal:

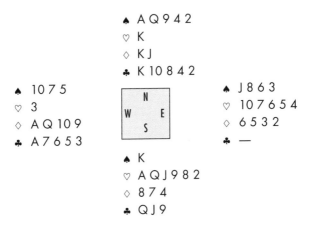

                        ♠ A Q 9 4 2
                        ♡ K
                        ◇ K J
                        ♣ K 10 8 4 2

    ♠ 10 7 5   ♠ J 8 6 3
    ♡ 3   ♡ 10 7 6 5 4
    ◇ A Q 10 9   ◇ 6 5 3 2
    ♣ A 7 6 5 3   ♣ —

                        ♠ K
                        ♡ A Q J 9 8 2
                        ◇ 8 7 4
                        ♣ Q J 9

I received a diamond lead and a diamond continuation. I overtook the
♡K with the ♡A, cashed a second heart to get the news in that suit,
and played on clubs. The defense was helpless. In 4♡, they can beat
us either by leading the ♣A to get two ruffs or by leading a trump. The
play in 5♣ is a little more complex, but that contract too will likely go
down.

Chapter 10

Balancing -or-
Boldly Going Where No Human Has Gone Before

*We had a partnership misunderstanding.
My partner assumed I knew
what I was doing.*

- Author unknown

A balancing action usually occurs after three passes, when the opponents have stopped at a low level despite finding a fit. Usually that means we also have a fit, with approximately one-half of the high cards. There are a number of factors to consider that may help to determine whether balancing is right.

Degree of Fit Found by the Opponents

Quite often, this is easy to determine, such as on an auction like 1♠ - 2♠ or 1♣ - 1♠; 2♠. However, sometimes the auction is ambiguous, for example 1♣ - 1♡; 1♠ - 2♣. You need to understand and know where you are in the auction. It is much safer to bid when the opponents are known to have a good fit than when they may not.

Matchpoints or Teams Scoring

At teams scoring, you want to be much more careful, especially vulnerable. Even not doubled, –200 vs. +50 is 6 IMPs away. At matchpoints you need to be more aggressive. At matchpoints, +110 is better than +50 or +100; of course, by the same token –90 is better than –100 in a two-level contract.

> **Tip 23** Sometimes it is better to come in early with a minimum hand, rather than wait to balance one level higher.

There are a couple of reasons for this. Firstly, the opponents have exchanged very little information. They will prefer to try and investigate their own fits and potential games or slams before doubling you. Secondly, if you wait, you will have to come in one level higher, and the chance that they will double is greater. Sometimes it is worth the risk to get a bid off your chest or to suggest a lead. There is risk, but there is also reward.

Here's an example where taking an early action is much safer. You hold as South:

♠ 5 3   ♡ 7 6 5   ◇ A K 9 8   ♣ K J 10 4

At matchpoints, East-West vulnerable, the bidding goes:

WEST	NORTH	EAST	SOUTH
		pass	pass
1♡	pass	1♠	?

Here you are a passed hand, so a double is pretty easy. Even if West had opened 1♡ in first chair, I would likely double because it is safer to do so now than at the three-level when the opponents have exchanged more information. However, this kind of 'pre-balancing' is more dangerous when you do not have the unbid suits.

BALANCING AGAINST 1NT

Many writers support Marty Bergen's dictum that it's never right to let the opponents play 1NT. But that simply isn't true, even at matchpoints. Look at this example.

North-South vulnerable at matchpoints, your hand as South is:

♠ A K 2 ♡ A J ◇ K 9 8 7 6 ♣ 8 7 6

The bidding goes:

WEST	NORTH	EAST	SOUTH
1NT[1]	pass	pass	?

1. 15-17.

Do you balance?

Your hand has a lot of high cards, but a poor suit. Also, you know that most of the high cards are sitting over yours. Pass. On the actual hand, partner had a 4-4-1-4 three-count, and you would go for –500 or –800.

This next case is a very different situation:

WEST	NORTH	EAST	SOUTH
1NT[1]	pass	pass	?

1. 15-17.

♠ K 10 9 6 5 3 ♡ 6 5 ◇ 5 2 ♣ 10 4 2

Do you balance with this hand?

Do you feel lucky? You should! Bid 2♠. The full deal from a recent Sectional:

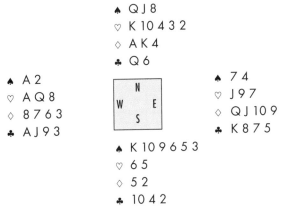

```
                    ♠ Q J 8
                    ♡ K 10 4 3 2
                    ◇ A K 4
                    ♣ Q 6
  ♠ A 2                                    ♠ 7 4
  ♡ A Q 8              N                   ♡ J 9 7
  ◇ 8 7 6 3        W       E               ◇ Q J 10 9
  ♣ A J 9 3            S                   ♣ K 8 7 5
                    ♠ K 10 9 6 5 3
                    ♡ 6 5
                    ◇ 5 2
                    ♣ 10 4 2
```

The difference is that partner is marked with points *over* the 1NT bidder, and you have a *good* six-card suit. It is more difficult for the opponents to double without values in your suit.

> *Bridge teaches you how to endure*
> *misery. It's not a game that can be*
> *played well, just in varying*
> *stages of badness.*
> – Edgar Kaplan

My last example is from our 2006 CNTC semifinal match against the eventual winner, Maksymetz, and was one of our few triumphs: Both vulnerable, you hold as North:

♠ 5 4 3 2 ♡ A Q 8 2 ◇ Q 5 ♣ A 10 2

WEST	NORTH	EAST	SOUTH
1♠	pass	2♠	pass
pass	?		

Do you bid, and if so, what?

I bid 3♡ and partner raised me to 4♡. I did not make a takeout double as partner is odds-on to hold some hearts, and I wanted to encourage a 4♡ call, as my hand has become much better on the auction. The full deal:

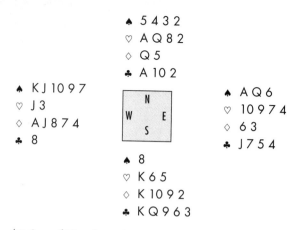

♠ 5 4 3 2
♡ A Q 8 2
◇ Q 5
♣ A 10 2

♠ K J 10 9 7
♡ J 3
◇ A J 8 7 4
♣ 8

N
W E
S

♠ A Q 6
♡ 10 9 7 4
◇ 6 3
♣ J 7 5 4

♠ 8
♡ K 6 5
◇ K 10 9 2
♣ K Q 9 6 3

We made 4♡ for +620, when the long clubs were with the long hearts. Please note Karl Gohl's excellent 4♡ call. Normally, a balance takes into account partner's values, but in this case Karl knew that I had to have *some* values to take a bid at all. Even if all I had was six hearts to the ace, there would be some play for game.

Chapter 11

GETTING OUT WHILE THE GETTING IS GOOD -OR- MISFITS

The real test of a bridge player
isn't in keeping out of trouble,
but in escaping once he's in.

\- Alfred Sheinwold

Successful bridge players get in the habit of listening to the opponents, both when they bid and when they are silent. Quite often the opponents' bidding will tell us that now is the time to be especially cautious. For example:

WEST	NORTH	EAST	SOUTH
2♡	dbl	pass	3♠
4♢	pass	pass	?

Your hand is:

♠ 9 7 6 4 ♡ K 5 2 ♢ K J ♣ A 5 3 2

Stay out! Sure, you have 11 HCP. But a likely distribution is:

```
              ♠ K Q 3 2
              ♡ 4 3
              ♢ A 8 5 4
              ♣ K J 7
  ♠ 5                        ♠ A J 10 8
  ♡ A J 10 9 8 6     N       ♡ Q 7
  ♢ Q 10 9 6     W     E     ♢ 7 3 2
  ♣ 8 6              S       ♣ Q 10 9 4
              ♠ 9 7 6 4
              ♡ K 5 2
              ♢ K J
              ♣ A 5 3 2
```

Fortunately, LHO rescued you. Don't jump back into the frying pan!

One of the hardest things to judge at the bridge table is when to get out when hands are misfitting. Often it is obvious from our own struggles in the bidding:

WEST	NORTH	EAST	SOUTH
pass	1♢	pass	1♠
pass	2♣	pass	3♠
pass	4♣		

These hands 'sound' like they are not fitting well. Another way of looking at misfit hands is that it is best to be cautious until a true fit is found, either by you or by the opponents.

You hold at IMPs:

♠ Q 10 9 7 5 ♡ Q ♢ J 10 8 5 2 ♣ Q 5

The bidding starts:

WEST	NORTH	EAST	SOUTH
pass	1♡	pass	1♠
pass	2♣	pass	?

Now is the time to quietly take a preference to partner's suit. You would like to able to do more, but for now, take it slowly. But let's say the bidding continues:

WEST	NORTH	EAST	SOUTH
pass	1♡	pass	1♠
pass	2♣	pass	2♡
pass	2♠	pass	?

All of a sudden things have changed! Instead of looking at a huge misfit, you have found a spade fit, and partner has a pretty good hand, usually around 14-17 HCP. What should you do?

I would bid 4♠. If you give partner a minimum hand for this auction, like

♠ A J 4   ♡ K J 9 8 6   ◇ 6   ♣ A J 8 2

then 4♠ is a pretty good contract. However, if he has

♠ A K 4   ♡ A K 8 7 4 2   ◇ 6   ♣ A 8 2

then 6♠ may make! Full speed ahead!

Tip 24 Imagine partner's hand opposite yours during the auction.

A useful technique is to visualize what partner might have for his bidding. Give him a hand, and then try to determine what is the best contract with this 'visualized' hand opposite yours.

> *South: Alert!*
> *East: Yes?*
> *South: I'm requested to further
> misdescribe my hand.*
> – Author unknown

Here is a hand I got wrong at the 2004 CNTC:

♠ J 9 7 ♡ 8 5 4 2 ◇ K ♣ K Q 9 6 5

I was North, and the bidding went:

WEST	NORTH	EAST	SOUTH
		2♡¹	dbl
pass	3♣²	pass	pass
3♡	4♣	all pass	

1. Five hearts and a five-card minor, 3-10 HCP.
2. Constructive, usually around 7-11 HCP.

I bid 4♣ as I thought my fifth club and distribution would fit well with partner's hand. However, if I had listened more carefully to the auction I would have detected the misfit. It seems that the opponents have a heart fit, yet West did not bid directly over the double, but instead balanced later with 3♡. Why? Also, partner passed my 3♣ despite its being encouraging.

The full deal:

```
                  ♠ J 9 7
                  ♡ 8 5 4 2
                  ◇ K
                  ♣ K Q 9 6 5
  ♠ Q 10 8 4 2          N          ♠ 3
  ♡ A 9 6         W         E       ♡ K J 10 7 3
  ◇ A Q 10 9 4          S          ◇ 6 2
  ♣ —                              ♣ 10 7 4 3 2
                  ♠ A K 6 5
                  ♡ Q
                  ◇ J 8 7 5 3
                  ♣ A J 8
```

My 4♣ contract went down three (I could have saved a trick, but I tried to make it) and 3♡ would have gone down a couple on a trump lead.

Chapter 12

ACCEPTING INVITATIONS –OR–
AM I DECLARER?

*One advantage of bad bidding
is that you get practice at
playing atrocious contracts.*

- Alfred Sheinwold

When to accept game invitations, it could be argued, is the meat and potatoes of judgment at bridge. There are many 6- and 10-IMP wins and losses resulting directly from whether you go to 4♠ or pass, following partner's 3♠ invitational bid. This chapter will try to capture some of the essence of the thinking that should go on prior to making the 'pass or bid on' decision.

> **Tip 25** You can win IMPs bidding bad games, and lose them bidding good ones.

Great games go down due to 5-0 or 4-1 trump breaks, and lousy games make when the ♠Q and ♠J in a 4♠ contract fall doubleton. That is life. What you want to do is improve your long-term success rate.

ISSUES TO CONSIDER WHEN DECIDING WHETHER TO ACCEPT A GAME INVITATION

TYPE OF SCORING

I say this a bit hesitatingly, as bridge is bridge. However, there is a greater reward for bidding vulnerable games at IMPs. In a pairs event, unless you are playing in a very strong field, bidding close games and going down (for whatever reason) will cost lots of matchpoints.

BIDDING BY THE OPPONENTS

This is a very important consideration. For example, let's say LHO opens 3♣ and partner overcalls 3♡. If you have an invitational hand with three small hearts, you know that there is good likelihood of a bad split behind partner's suit. On the other hand, *the opponents' bidding always helps you place cards*. If someone opens a preempt, the other hand will usually have most of the high cards. If an opponent makes a 2♢ overcall, he has a certain minimum in high card points and at least five diamonds. You 'know' that ♢AQ5 over him is as good as ♢AK5, as the overcaller will have the ♢K 99% of the time. Even ♢AQ10 will often be as good as ♢AKQ for the same reason. Think about all of the great declarer play examples that you read about in bridge articles. They *all* have one thing in common—the opponents have bid, pointing the way to success!

BID CLOSE GAMES WHEN YOU KNOW ONE OPPONENT HAS MOST, IF NOT ALL, OF THE HIGH CARDS

This is usually like playing double dummy. You can often endplay or squeeze the hand with all of the high cards.

The 2003 Wagar final went to an 8-board playoff when the teams were tied after the fourth quarter. This was a key pick-up for the Eythorsdottir team.

As South you hold:

♠ A K 2 ♡ K J 10 3 ◇ Q 9 2 ♣ J 6 3

WEST	NORTH	EAST	SOUTH
		1♣[1]	pass
1◇[2]	pass	1♡	pass
pass	dbl	pass	?

1. Precision, 16+ HCP, any distribution.
2. 0-7 HCP.

```
                    ♠ 10 5 3
                    ♡ 6 5
                    ◇ K 10 4
                    ♣ A Q 9 7 4
    ♠ 9 7 6 4                      ♠ Q J 8
    ♡ 7 2          ┌─────┐         ♡ A Q 9 8 4
    ◇ 8 7 6 5      │  N  │         ◇ A J 3
    ♣ 10 5 2     W │     │ E       ♣ K 8
                   │  S  │
                   └─────┘
                    ♠ A K 2
                    ♡ K J 10 3
                    ◇ Q 9 2
                    ♣ J 6 3
```

Here, Tobi Sokolow knew partner Janice Seamon-Molson had 9-10 HCP, West had 0-1 HCP, and East 16-17 with five hearts. This should have meant bidding 3NT, similar to the bid made by Kerri Sanborn with her cards in the other room, instead of the 1NT bid she actually made at the table. She should have realized that her heart holding may well be worth as much as ♡AKQ—good for three tricks—and that the hand can be played double dummy with likely squeeze and endplay possibilities.

LOOK AT YOUR SPOT CARDS

Spot cards, especially in the trump suit, come in handy when trying to overcome bad splits, and give you two-way finessing choices. If you are thinking about playing in a 4-3 trump fit, the four-card holding should be strong, as you usually need the three-card holding to ruff losers. So ♠J1098 is good, ♠J1086 is okay, and ♠J743 is bad.

This is a similar kind of situation. You hold as South:

♠ Q 9 8 4 3 ♡ J 7 5 ◊ K 6 ♣ 10 4 2

Playing teams, both vulnerable, the bidding has gone:

WEST	NORTH	EAST	SOUTH
		pass	pass
1♣	1♡	1NT	pass
2♣	dbl	3♣	?

It was a close decision as to whether or not to bid 2♡. Now, partner is showing a good hand for an overcall with support for the unbid suits. This time it is close between 3♠ and 4♠.

You have a fifth spade, support for hearts and great diamonds. At teams, I would bid four to take the pressure off partner. Three sounds competitive, and could be bid with less. The full deal:

```
              ♠ A K 10 2
              ♡ A Q 9 4 2
              ◊ Q 9 7 5
              ♣ —
  ♠ 6                        ♠ J 7 5
  ♡ 8 3          N           ♡ K 10 6
  ◊ A 4 3 2    W   E         ◊ J 10 8
  ♣ K Q J 9 8 7    S         ♣ A 6 5 3
              ♠ Q 9 8 4 3
              ♡ J 7 5
              ◊ K 6
              ♣ 10 4 2
```

Again, it is important to recognize the value of the good spade spots in your hand, especially if partner has only three trumps. The reason for this is you will have to take ruffs in the short hand.

DEGREE OF FIT

If partner opens the bidding with 1◇ and raises your 1♠ to 3♠, I would bid game with

♠ K 9 5 2   ♡ 8 7   ◇ K J 9   ♣ 9 7 6 4

because you know that your diamond cards are working. An average hand for partner:

♠ A Q 8 6   ♡ 9 4 2   ◇ A 10 8 3 2   ♣ A

LOOK AT YOUR HIGH CARDS

The standard 4-3-2-1 point count is easy to apply, but it undervalues aces and kings, and overvalues queens and jacks. So don't just count your points, look at the type of high cards you have.

You hold as South:

♠ 5   ♡ K J 10 2   ◇ K J 4   ♣ A Q 9 8 7

The bidding goes:

WEST	NORTH	EAST	SOUTH
pass	pass	pass	1♣
pass	1♠	pass	2♣
pass	3♠	pass	?

Pass. But bid game with:

♠ Q 5   ♡ A 7 3 2   ◇ K 4   ♣ A 9 8 4 3

The difference is fast versus slow points (aces as opposed to queens and jacks) and the degree of fit. Partner's invitational 3♠ will likely be based on something like:

♠ K J 9 7 4 3 2   ♡ 6 5   ◇ A 9 8   ♣ 5

> *If I did everything right, I*
> *wouldn't be playing with you.*
> – Author unknown

NUMBER OF TRUMPS

As has been mentioned previously, the Law of Total Tricks has been the topic of many books over the last few years. Essentially, a nine- or ten-card fit is significantly better than an eight-card fit.

You hold:

♠ 6 4 ♡ K 10 9 7 6 4 ◇ Q 9 8 7 3 ♣ —

The bidding goes:

WEST	NORTH	EAST	SOUTH
pass	1♣	pass	1♡
pass	2♡	pass	?

Partner almost certainly has four hearts, and you will be able to ruff diamonds if necessary. I would bid 4♡. Even if partner has a disgusting non-fitting hand like

♠ Q 8 7 ♡ Q 5 3 2 ◇ A ♣ K J 8 7 3

the heart game still has a play. If instead he has

♠ A 7 ♡ A 5 3 2 ◇ K J ♣ 9 8 7 3 2

then 6♡ is cold on a non-spade lead.

COUNT YOUR TRICKS

If you have a good idea that you have enough tricks for it, bid game.

STATE OF THE MATCH

You never want to try to predict how well a match is going, but one strategy to create swings is to try to bid differently than the opponents. This might mean accepting sub-par results and perhaps losing by a lot, in the hope that the bridge gods are kind to you on a particular deal. The following is a more drastic strategy.

You hold as North:

♠ J 8 ♡ 10 9 4 2 ◇ A K Q J 10 8 7 ♣ —

WEST	NORTH	EAST	SOUTH
		1♠	2♡
3♣	?		

There are a number of natural and tactical bids that could be made with this hand, the most logical being 3◇.

Michael Rosenberg, at the 1999 NABC in Vancouver, found a tactical bid that worked exactly as he planned. He bid 5♠, Exclusion Blackwood! His partner Zia held

♠ 10 5 ♡ A K J 8 5 3 ◇ 6 5 4 ♣ Q 4

and showed two keycards outside the spade suit. Rosenberg bid 7♡ over the opposition's 6♠ bid. They led the ♣A and 7♡ made when hearts split 2-1.

Actually, Michael was ahead of his time. With the current popularity of poker, especially Texas Hold'em, many would recognize this as an 'all in' move.

INVITING GAMES—NOT!

The above tips and guidelines are all valid in helping you judge whether to make and accept invitations. However, there are some other psychological reasons why in certain situations you should just bid game.

> **Tip 26** Think about all the factors when deciding whether to invite or not.

It has been commonly held that certain hands fall within the invitation boundaries. For example, you hold:

♠ 5 4 ♡ A Q 10 7 ◇ 9 7 6 5 ♣ K 3 2

Partner opens a 15-17 notrump and you would usually invite by using Stayman, then raising 2♡ to 3♡ or bidding 2NT over either 2◇ or 2♠. However, there are times when you may want to gamble on game anyway. Maybe you decide to shoot for a good score, or maybe partner will not be able to make an intelligent decision as to whether he has what you need.

Let's say you have:

♠ A 10 9 7 5 2 ♡ 4 ◇ Q 10 9 6 5 ♣ 4

WEST	NORTH	EAST	SOUTH
	1♣	pass	1♠
pass	2♠	pass	?

If you make a game try with 3♢, partner may sign off with a minimum when game is cold. Even without giving him an actual opening bid, say,

♠ K 8 6 4   ♡ A 9 8 7   ♢ 6   ♣ Q 8 7 5

—only 9 HCP—game is cold with normal breaks.

To be honest, I would still invite game on this hand. However, there are a number of other advantages to just bidding game.

THE OPPONENTS MAY NOT MAKE A CLOSE DOUBLE

You are East, holding:

♠ 3   ♡ K Q 10 9   ♢ Q J 10 9   ♣ Q 10 9 8

The bidding goes at matchpoints:

WEST	NORTH	EAST	SOUTH
pass	1NT	pass	2♣
pass	2♡	pass	2NT
pass	3NT	?	

Double! The full deal is:

```
              ♠ 7 6 4
              ♡ A J 5 2
              ♢ A K 3
              ♣ A J 3
  ♠ K J 9 8 2      N       ♠ 3
  ♡ 8 4 3      W       E   ♡ K Q 10 9
  ♢ 6 4            S       ♢ Q J 10 9
  ♣ 6 5 4                  ♣ Q 10 9 8
              ♠ A Q 10 5
              ♡ 7 6
              ♢ 8 7 5 2
              ♣ K 7 2
```

Okay, okay, I confess that I made this hand up. But it still illustrates that the opponents are down -800, despite having 26 HCP between them.

Now let's say the bidding just went 1NT-3NT. Now if you double, on the same 'Where are their tricks coming from?' rationale, the full deal might be:

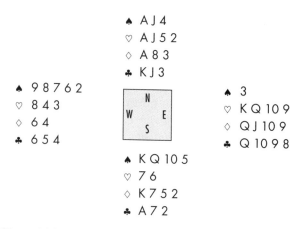

Now 3NT could have nine top tricks. In fact, your double has high-lighted where all the points are, and declarer will likely make six or seven, as you are squeezed to a pulp on the run of the spades. In case you've never seen this number, 3NT vulnerable doubled making six is –1350!

> *We believe that contract bridge is*
> *particularly attractive to people*
> *with a scrappy disposition.*
> – Frank Perkins

THE OPPONENTS DON'T KNOW WHETHER THEY SHOULD BE DEFENDING PASSIVELY OR NOT

A more hesitant auction will usually inspire a more conservative lead and defense. Again, this is best illustrated by an example.

Playing IMPs, sitting South, both sides vulnerable, your hand is:

♠ Q 10 2 ♡ 10 7 4 2 ◇ K 3 ♣ Q 9 8 2

The bidding has gone:

WEST	NORTH	EAST	SOUTH
		1♠	pass
2♠	pass	2NT	pass
4♠	all pass		

What do you lead? Most people, if asked, would likely lead a small heart. It doesn't sound like the opponents have anything extra, so there is no reason to make a risky lead that could blow a trick.

The full deal might be:

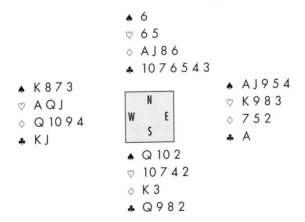

```
              ♠ 4
              ♡ A 6 5 3
              ◊ J 9 8 6 4 2
              ♣ A 10
  ♠ 9 6 5 3                    ♠ A K J 8 7
  ♡ J 9 8        N             ♡ K Q
  ◊ A 7       W     E          ◊ Q 10 5
  ♣ K 6 4 3      S             ♣ J 7 5
              ♠ Q 10 2
              ♡ 10 7 4 2
              ◊ K 3
              ♣ Q 9 8 2
```

Let's imagine you have the same hand, but now the bidding goes:

WEST	NORTH	EAST	SOUTH
		1♠	pass
2NT[1]	pass	3♣[2]	pass
3♡	pass	4♣	pass
4♠	all pass		

1. Game-forcing spade raise.
2. Singleton club.

Now you lead the ◊K. Again you are rewarded:

```
              ♠ 6
              ♡ 6 5
              ◊ A J 8 6
              ♣ 10 7 6 5 4 3
  ♠ K 8 7 3                    ♠ A J 9 5 4
  ♡ A Q J        N             ♡ K 9 8 3
  ◊ Q 10 9 4  W     E          ◊ 7 5 2
  ♣ K J         S              ♣ A
              ♠ Q 10 2
              ♡ 10 7 4 2
              ◊ K 3
              ♣ Q 9 8 2
```

YOU DON'T GIVE AWAY DISTRIBUTIONAL OR HIGH CARD INFORMATION

If you are always going to bid game—bid it! If it is close, you may want to bid it anyway.

Playing teams, both sides vulnerable, you hold as South:

♠ — ♡ 9 8 3 ◇ A K J 8 3 ♣ J 10 9 7 5

The bidding goes:

WEST	NORTH	EAST	SOUTH
			pass
pass	1♡	pass	?

Bid 4♡! Yes, there is a possibility you might have a slam, but partner will probably bid again if that is the case. If not, you want to play in 4♡. By splintering or bidding diamonds, you are just giving away valuable information that will aid the opponents' defense. They will also benefit from your partner's next call.

THE OPPONENTS MAY TAKE A SACRIFICE AGAINST YOUR CONFIDENT AUCTION

As a result, their partners may be +140 or +170 in 3♠ making, while at your table they have sacrificed and gone down –300 or –500 to lose 4 or 8 IMPs. A slower auction gives more information to the opponents and lets them make better decisions. Say the auction goes:

WEST	NORTH	EAST	SOUTH
		1♠	pass
2♠	pass	3♣	pass
3◇	pass	3NT	pass
4♠	all pass		

A very revealing auction! It appears that East has five spades, and is short in diamonds with a secondary club suit. From

♠ 10 6 5 ♡ A 2 ◇ 8 7 4 ♣ Q 9 7 5 2

you will probably lead a trump. However, if the auction had gone 1♠ - 2♠; 4♠, the ♡A or a diamond are both reasonable leads, and both would allow 4♠ to make!

The full deal:

```
                    ♠ 9 7
                    ♡ J 7 6 5
                    ◇ K 10 9 3
                    ♣ A 8 4
  ♠ K 4 3          ┌─────────┐        ♠ A Q J 8 2
  ♡ 9 8 4 3        │    N    │        ♡ K Q 10
  ◇ A Q J 6 5      │ W     E │        ◇ 2
  ♣ 6              │    S    │        ♣ K J 10 3
                   └─────────┘
                    ♠ 10 6 5
                    ♡ A 2
                    ◇ 8 7 4
                    ♣ Q 9 7 5 2
```

Chapter 13

Now It's Your Turn -or-
Did I Waste My Money on This Book!?

*Learn from the mistakes of others.
You won't live long enough to
make them all yourself.*

- Alfred Sheinwold

One word about the following problems. I chose not to tell you which chapter each problem is testing. Just like at the bridge table… In each case, you have to choose the next bid or call.

PROBLEMS

PROBLEM 1

Both vulnerable at IMPs, as South you hold:

♠ A K 9 7 5   ♡ K 9   ◇ Q 10 8 6 4 3   ♣ —

WEST	NORTH	EAST	SOUTH
pass	1◇	3♡	4♡
5♣	5♠	6♣	6◇
6♡	pass	pass	?

PROBLEM 2

North-South vulnerable at IMPs, as South you hold:

♠ 10 9 3   ♡ K 6   ◇ K 10 9 2   ♣ K J 9 4

WEST	NORTH	EAST	SOUTH
		pass	pass
2♠	dbl	3♠	4◇
pass	4♡	pass	?

PROBLEM 3

Neither vulnerable at IMPs, as South you hold:

♠ A K 2   ♡ A 10   ◇ K Q J 9 5   ♣ A 10 5

WEST	NORTH	EAST	SOUTH
1♡	pass	3♡[1]	dbl
pass	5♣	pass	?

1. Preemptive.

PROBLEM 4

Both vulnerable at IMPs, as South you hold:

♠ J 10 8 ♡ A Q 8 4 3 2 ◇ A ♣ A 8 2

WEST	NORTH	EAST	SOUTH
	1NT¹	pass	2◇²
pass	2♡	pass	4◇³
dbl	redbl⁴	pass	?

1. 15-17.
2. Transfer.
3. Splinter slam try.
4. Second-round diamond control. Denies a terrible hand for hearts (but it sure is close to that!).

PROBLEM 5

Both vulnerable at IMPs, as South you hold:

♠ Q 10 8 7 6 5 3 ♡ K 5 ◇ 10 7 3 ♣ 8

WEST	NORTH	EAST	SOUTH
1♣	pass	1♡	2♠
3♠	4♠	5♡	?

PROBLEM 6

East-West vulnerable at matchpoints, as South you hold:

♠ A ♡ Q 7 5 2 ◇ A ♣ A Q J 10 7 4 2

WEST	NORTH	EAST	SOUTH
2♡	3◇	3♡	?

Since the average person's small supply of politeness must last him all his life, they can't afford to waste it on bridge partners.
— Alfred Sheinwold

PROBLEM 7

East-West vulnerable at matchpoints, as South you hold:

♠ Q 8 3　♡ K Q 7 2　◇ 8 3　♣ A 10 8 3

WEST	NORTH	EAST	SOUTH
	pass	pass	1♣
1◇	1♠	pass	pass
2◇	dbl	3♣	?

PROBLEM 8

Both vulnerable at IMPs, as South you hold:

♠ A　♡ K 10 9 6 4　◇ 4　♣ A K Q 9 7 5

WEST	NORTH	EAST	SOUTH
		1◇	?

PROBLEM 9

North-South vulnerable at matchpoints, as North you hold:

♠ J 8 4 3　♡ 10 7 5　◇ A J 5 2　♣ K 7

WEST	NORTH	EAST	SOUTH
pass	pass	1♡	1♠
pass	2♡¹	3♡	pass
pass	?		

1. Limit raise in spades.

> *Success is a matter of luck—*
> *just ask any failure.*
> – Anonymous

PROBLEM 10

Both vulnerable at IMPs, as North you hold:

♠ K 4 2 ♡ J 10 8 7 2 ◇ Q 7 ♣ 10 9 5

WEST	NORTH	EAST	SOUTH
pass	pass	1♣	dbl
pass	1♡	pass	2♣
pass	?		

PROBLEM 11

North-South vulnerable at IMPs, as South you hold:

♠ 6 ♡ J 4 ◇ A K Q J 10 6 4 ♣ J 9 4

WEST	NORTH	EAST	SOUTH
		pass	?

PROBLEM 12

Both vulnerable at IMPs, as South you hold:

♠ A K 9 7 4 ♡ A K 2 ◇ K 2 ♣ Q J 2

WEST	NORTH	EAST	SOUTH
	pass	1♠	pass
1NT	pass	2♣	pass
2◇	pass	pass	?

PROBLEM 13

Both vulnerable at IMPs, as South you hold:

♠ A 6 ♡ K 9 ◇ A K 8 7 6 2 ♣ A J 8

WEST	NORTH	EAST	SOUTH
	3♠	pass	?

PROBLEM 14

East-West vulnerable at matchpoints, as South you hold:

♠ K 9 7 6 ♡ A 9 8 5 4 3 ◇ 10 ♣ 5 2

WEST	NORTH	EAST	SOUTH
pass	pass	1◇	1♡
pass	pass	dbl	pass
1NT	pass	pass	?

PROBLEM 15

Both vulnerable at IMPs, as South you hold:

♠ K 7 ♡ A Q 7 ◇ A 8 6 4 ♣ A 8 5 2

WEST	NORTH	EAST	SOUTH
1♠	pass	2♠	dbl
pass	4♡	4♠	?

PROBLEM 16

Both vulnerable at IMPs, as North you hold:

♠ 9 6 5 2 ♡ Q 8 6 2 ◇ A 7 6 2 ♣ 3

WEST	NORTH	EAST	SOUTH
pass	pass	2◇[1]	3◇
4◇	dbl	4♡	pass
pass	?		

1. 11-15 HCP, three-suiter short in diamonds (could be 3-4 or 4-3 in majors).

> *Do what you can, with*
> *what you have, where you are.*
> – Theodore Roosevelt

PROBLEM 17

North-South vulnerable at matchpoints, as South you hold:

♠ K 9 6 5 ♡ J 10 7 3 2 ◇ 6 4 ♣ K 8

WEST	NORTH	EAST	SOUTH
		pass	pass
1♡	2♣	2♡	?

PROBLEM 18

Both vulnerable at IMPs, as West you hold:

♠ Q 6 2 ♡ K 9 7 3 ◇ A K 3 ♣ 4 3 2

WEST	NORTH	EAST	SOUTH
			1♠
pass	2♠¹	pass	pass
?			

1. Weak two-level raise.

PROBLEM 19

Both vulnerable at IMPs, as South you hold:

♠ Q 9 6 4 3 ♡ A K 7 4 3 ◇ K Q 8 ♣ —

WEST	NORTH	EAST	SOUTH
pass	1◇	pass	1♠
pass	2◇	pass	2♡
pass	2♠	pass	?

It's not the skill that drops off with age,
it's the drive, the killer instinct...
and when a player isn't primed
to kill, they make mistakes.
– Author unknown

PROBLEM 20

Both vulnerable at IMPs, as South you hold:

♠ J 5 4 3 ♡ Q 9 5 ◇ A 6 ♣ A K 8 6

WEST	NORTH	EAST	SOUTH
1◇	pass	pass	dbl
pass	1♠	pass	?

PROBLEM 21

East-West vulnerable at IMPs, as South you hold:

♠ A K Q 8 4 3 2 ♡ A Q ◇ 4 2 ♣ 9 6

WEST	NORTH	EAST	SOUTH
1♡	pass	1NT	?

PROBLEM 22

Neither vulnerable at IMPs, as South you hold:

♠ — ♡ Q 7 2 ◇ A Q 10 9 6 5 4 ♣ A 8 4

WEST	NORTH	EAST	SOUTH
1♠	3♡[1]	4♠	?

1. Preemptive.

PROBLEM 23

Neither vulnerable at IMPs, as South you hold:

♠ Q ♡ K J 6 ◇ A Q 10 5 4 3 ♣ A Q J

WEST	NORTH	EAST	SOUTH
pass	pass	2♡	?

PROBLEM 24

Both vulnerable at IMPs, as South you hold:

♠ K J 10 2 ♡ Q J 7 ◇ A 7 4 3 2 ♣ 6

WEST	NORTH	EAST	SOUTH
			1◇
pass	1♡	pass	?

PROBLEM 25

Neither vulnerable at IMPs, as South you hold:

♠ 5 ♡ 4 2 ◇ A Q 9 ♣ A K Q 10 9 8 3

WEST	NORTH	EAST	SOUTH
			1♣
2♡	2♠	4♡	5♣
pass	5♠	pass	?

PROBLEM 26

North-South vulnerable at matchpoints, as South you hold:

♠ 9 7 ♡ A K Q 10 9 8 7 5 4 ◇ — ♣ J 5

WEST	NORTH	EAST	SOUTH
pass	1◇	pass	1♡
pass	2♣	pass	?

> *Deadly accuracy in bidding*
> *is hard to beat!*
> - Omar Sharif

PROBLEM 27

Neither vulnerable at IMPs, as South you hold:

♠ A 10 9 8 6 ♡ 8 ◇ Q 5 2 ♣ J 8 5 2

WEST	NORTH	EAST	SOUTH
			pass
pass	pass	1♡	1♠
2♣	2♡	pass	2♠
3♡	3♠	4♡	pass
pass	dbl	pass	?

PROBLEM 28

North-South vulnerable at IMPs, as South you hold:

♠ 3 2 ♡ 7 6 5 ◇ Q 9 5 3 2 ♣ A Q 7

WEST	NORTH	EAST	SOUTH
1♡	dbl	4♡	?

PROBLEM 29

East-West vulnerable at IMPs, as South you hold:

♠ 10 8 3 2 ♡ 9 8 ◇ 8 5 3 ♣ A Q J 10

WEST	NORTH	EAST	SOUTH
			pass
pass	1♠	pass	2♠
pass	3◇	pass	3♠
pass	4♣	pass	?

> *Your play was better tonight,*
> *and so were your excuses.*
> – Author unknown

PROBLEM 30

North-South vulnerable at IMPs, as South you hold:

♠ A 10 9 8 6 2 ♡ 8 ◇ K J 9 7 ♣ K Q

WEST	NORTH	EAST	SOUTH
1◇	1♠	dbl	4♠
5◇	5♠	pass	?

PROBLEM 31

Neither vulnerable at IMPs, as South you hold:

♠ K Q 9 3 2 ♡ A Q J 9 8 4 3 ◇ — ♣ 8

WEST	NORTH	EAST	SOUTH
	pass	pass	1♡
2NT	pass	3◇	3♠
5◇	dbl	pass	?

PROBLEM 32

North-South vulnerable at IMPs, as South you hold:

♠ A J ♡ A 2 ◇ K Q 10 7 6 5 ♣ A 9 7

WEST	NORTH	EAST	SOUTH
	pass	1♠	dbl
4♠	5♡	dbl	?

PROBLEM 33

Neither vulnerable at IMPs, as South you hold:

♠ 3 2 ♡ 9 ◇ A Q 9 8 ♣ Q 10 9 8 7 2

WEST	NORTH	EAST	SOUTH
	1♡	1NT	?

PROBLEM 34

Both vulnerable at IMPs, as South you hold:

♠ 6 5 ♡ A J 10 9 3 ◇ K 10 ♣ A Q 10 5

WEST	NORTH	EAST	SOUTH
pass	pass	1♡	pass
1♠	pass	pass	dbl
pass	1NT	pass	?

PROBLEM 35

North-South vulnerable at IMPs, as South you hold:

♠ A Q 10 3 2 ♡ A K J ◇ — ♣ A Q 8 6 2

WEST	NORTH	EAST	SOUTH
pass	pass	4◇	?

PROBLEM 36

East-West vulnerable at IMPs, as South you hold:

♠ Q 6 5 3 2 ♡ K 7 ◇ 7 ♣ 9 7 4 3 2

WEST	NORTH	EAST	SOUTH
	1♣	1◇	1♠
2♣	pass	2♡	?

PROBLEM 37

Neither vulnerable at IMPs, as South you hold:

♠ A K Q 8 4 ♡ 10 5 ◇ J 8 3 ♣ A Q 4

WEST	NORTH	EAST	SOUTH
	1◇	pass	1♠
pass	2◇	pass	3♣
pass	3♡	pass	3NT
pass	4♠	pass	?

PROBLEM 38

East-West vulnerable at IMPs, as South you hold:

♠ A Q 3 ♡ J 10 9 6 5 ◇ K 10 4 ♣ A Q

WEST	NORTH	EAST	SOUTH
		2♠	?

PROBLEM 39

East-West vulnerable at IMPs, as South you hold:

♠ A K 4 ♡ A K 9 5 ◇ 8 4 ♣ 9 7 6 2

WEST	NORTH	EAST	SOUTH
		1◇	1♡ 1
pass	4◇ 2	dbl	4♠
pass	5♣	dbl	?

1. Double is a better bid, but I was trying to do something a little different.
2. Splinter.

> *In order to get to the*
> *fruit of the tree you have to*
> *go out on the limb.*
> – Shirley MacLaine

PROBLEM 40

Neither vulnerable at IMPs, as South you hold:

♠ J 7 3 ♡ 7 5 4 ◇ 7 4 3 2 ♣ A K 5

WEST	NORTH	EAST	SOUTH
	1♡	pass	2♡ 1
3♣	3◇ 2	pass	?

1. 6-9 pts, 3-card support.
2. Length in diamonds, game try (focus on diamond fit and aces and kings in other suits).

PROBLEM 41

North-South vulnerable at IMPs, as West you hold:

♠ A Q 9 5 2 ♡ J 2 ◇ A K Q 4 ♣ J 6

WEST	NORTH	EAST	SOUTH
	2♡	pass	3♣
3♠	4◇	4♠	pass
pass	5♣	pass	pass
?			

PROBLEM 42

North-South vulnerable at IMPs, as West you hold:

♠ A Q J 10 7 ♡ A K Q 10 2 ◇ A 9 3 ♣ —

WEST	NORTH	EAST	SOUTH
2♣	pass	2◇¹	pass
2♠	pass	2NT	pass
3♡	pass	3NT	pass
?			

1. Waiting.

PROBLEM 43

East-West vulnerable at IMPs, as South you hold:

♠ K 7 6 ♡ 8 ◇ A J 9 5 4 3 ♣ A 10 3

WEST	NORTH	EAST	SOUTH
			1◇
pass	1♡	1♠	2◇
2♠	3◇	3♡	pass
3♠	pass	pass	?

PROBLEM 44

Both vulnerable at IMPs, as South you hold:

♠ K 8 6 4 3 ♡ A K Q J ◇ J 5 ♣ 5 2

WEST	NORTH	EAST	SOUTH
			1♠
pass	1NT	2◇	2♡
pass	3♡	4◇	pass
pass	dbl	pass	?

PROBLEM 45

Neither vulnerable at IMPs, as West you hold:

♠ Q 5 2 ♡ 8 4 3 2 ◇ K 9 ♣ K Q 8 6

WEST	NORTH	EAST	SOUTH
pass	pass	1♣	1♡
dbl	pass	2♡	pass
3♣	pass	3♠	pass
?			

PROBLEM 46

East-West vulnerable at IMPs, as East you hold:

♠ A Q 10 9 7 6 ♡ K Q 9 ◇ 5 ♣ Q 8 2

WEST	NORTH	EAST	SOUTH
			1♡
2NT	3♣[1]	?	

1. Limit raise in hearts.

> *The difference between success and*
> *failure at anything is*
> *often slim.*
> - Anonymous

PROBLEM 47

Neither vulnerable at IMPs, as North you hold:

♠ K 7 3 ♡ A 7 6 5 4 2 ◇ K 7 ♣ A 2

WEST	NORTH	EAST	SOUTH
	1♡	pass	2♣
2♠	pass	pass	3◇
pass	?		

PROBLEM 48

Both vulnerable at IMPs, as South you hold:

♠ 10 4 3 ♡ Q ◇ 8 7 3 ♣ A Q 10 9 4 2

WEST	NORTH	EAST	SOUTH
	1♠	dbl	2♡¹
dbl	2♠	pass	?

1. Constructive spade raise.

PROBLEM 49

North-South vulnerable at IMPs, as North you hold:

♠ A K Q 8 4 ♡ A J 9 6 5 ◇ 8 3 ♣ A

WEST	NORTH	EAST	SOUTH
		pass	1◇
pass	1♠	pass	2◇
pass	2♡	pass	3◇
pass	?		

PROBLEM 50

North-South vulnerable at IMPs, as South you hold:

♠ A K 4 ♡ Q 10 9 8 4 ◇ 8 ♣ 7 5 4 2

WEST	NORTH	EAST	SOUTH
3♠	dbl	pass	4♡
pass	4♠	pass	?

PROBLEM 51

North-South vulnerable at IMPs, as South you hold:

♠ A 10 4 3 ♡ A K 5 ◇ 10 9 3 ♣ Q 9 4

WEST	NORTH	EAST	SOUTH
			1NT[1]
pass	4◇[2]	4♠	?

1. 12-14 HCP.
2. Transfer to hearts.

PROBLEM 52

North-South vulnerable at IMPs, as West you hold:

♠ J 10 6 5 4 ♡ A 10 5 ◇ Q J 5 3 ♣ A

WEST	NORTH	EAST	SOUTH
			1♠
pass	pass	2♡	3♠
?			

> *Most people think only once or twice a year. I have made myself an international reputation by thinking once or twice a week.*
> – George Bernard Shaw

PROBLEM 53

North-South vulnerable at IMPs, as South you hold:

♠ J 7 3 2 ♡ A 9 4 ◇ — ♣ A K 7 5 4 3

WEST	NORTH	EAST	SOUTH
2♠¹	pass	3◇	pass
pass	4♠	pass	?

1. A weak preempt in any suit.

PROBLEM 54

Both vulnerable at IMPs, as South you hold:

♠ A ♡ K Q ◇ K J 8 5 4 3 ♣ A 10 8 6

WEST	NORTH	EAST	SOUTH
			1◇
pass	1♠	pass	2♣
pass	2♡	pass	3◇
pass	3NT	pass	?

PROBLEM 55

North-South vulnerable at IMPs, as North you hold:

♠ A K 9 3 ♡ Q ◇ A J 8 7 2 ♣ 9 8 2

WEST	NORTH	EAST	SOUTH
	1◇	pass	1♡
pass	1♠	pass	2♣¹
pass	2◇	pass	2♡
pass	3♣	pass	3◇
pass	?		

1. Fourth suit, game forcing.

PROBLEM 56

North-South vulnerable at IMPs, as West you hold:

♠ 4 2 ♡ A K Q 4 ◇ K 10 7 ♣ Q 9 6 2

WEST	NORTH	EAST	SOUTH
	pass	pass	1♠
dbl	2NT[1]	3♡	3♠
?			

1. Limit raise in spades.

PROBLEM 57

Neither vulnerable at IMPs, as North you hold:

♠ 9 7 6 4 ♡ 3 ◇ J 8 2 ♣ J 8 7 6 2

WEST	NORTH	EAST	SOUTH
		2♡	dbl
3♣[1]	pass	3♡	3♠
4♡	4♠	pass	pass
5♡	?		

1. Lead-directing.

PROBLEM 58

Both vulnerable at IMPs, as South you hold:

♠ A 7 6 5 3 ♡ A K 10 9 4 ◇ 3 ♣ K 4

WEST	NORTH	EAST	SOUTH
	1♣	pass	1♠
dbl	2◇	pass	2♡
pass	2NT	pass	3♡
pass	3NT	pass	?

PROBLEM 59

East-West vulnerable at IMPs, as South you hold:

♠ Q 8 2 ♡ K 9 7 3 ◊ Q 2 ♣ 5 4 3 2

WEST	NORTH	EAST	SOUTH
			pass
pass	1◊	pass	1♡
pass	3♣	pass	3◊
pass	3♡	pass	?

PROBLEM 60

Both vulnerable at IMPs, as South you hold:

♠ A 4 ♡ A K Q 8 5 ◊ — ♣ A K 10 4 3 2

WEST	NORTH	EAST	SOUTH
			?

What is your call?

PROBLEM 61

Both vulnerable at IMPs, as South you hold:

♠ K 4 ♡ A Q 7 ◊ J 8 7 4 2 ♣ K Q 10

WEST	NORTH	EAST	SOUTH
1♣	pass	1♡	?

PROBLEM 62

East-West vulnerable at IMPs, as South you hold:

♠ — ♡ Q J 10 ◊ A 10 8 7 6 5 ♣ K 8 6 4

WEST	NORTH	EAST	SOUTH
1♠	pass	pass	dbl
2♡	dbl	3♠	pass
pass	dbl	pass	?

PROBLEM 63

Neither vulnerable at IMPs, as West you hold:

♠ A K 10   ♡ 10 8 7   ◇ A K J 8 7 4   ♣ 7

WEST	NORTH	EAST	SOUTH
1◇	4♡	5◇	
?			pass

SOLUTIONS

SOLUTION 1

Both vulnerable at IMPs, as South you hold:

♠ A K 9 7 5   ♡ K 9   ◇ Q 10 8 6 4 3   ♣ —

WEST	NORTH	EAST	SOUTH
pass	1◇	3♡	4♡
5♣	5♠	6♣	6◇
6♡	pass	pass	?

Bid 7◇ or 7♠. This hand was the talk of the 2004 CNTC in St. Catharines. Some experts might choose to bid 3♠ instead of 4♡, but I thought it was important to show my prime diamond support and heart control. The advantage of bidding 4♡ is that you still will likely have the opportunity to bid spades over any heart bids, thus painting a pretty accurate picture of your hand. But your partner beat you to it with his 5♠ bid!

In my view, 5♠ on this auction should be natural, as the opponents have bid the other two suits naturally (yes, 5♣ may be only lead-directing).

North's thinking is that this should help our partnership make the right decision over the inevitable 6♡.

The key bid is partner's pass of 6♡, showing a first-round heart control and inviting 7◇. He doesn't know about your spades. For his aggressive bidding, he must have the ◇AK. Bid seven confidently. I would choose 7◇ because of the lower likelihood of a spade ruff, but would bid spades over a 7♡ sacrifice.

> *I'm not sure whether glory*
> *or masterpoints is first on the list,*
> *but I know learning to play*
> *better is definitely last.*
> *- Eddie Kantar*

The full deal:

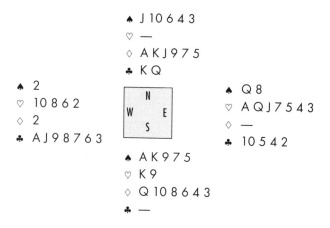

```
                   ♠ J 10 6 4 3
                   ♡ —
                   ◇ A K J 9 7 5
                   ♣ K Q
    ♠ 2                              ♠ Q 8
    ♡ 10 8 6 2        N              ♡ A Q J 7 5 4 3
    ◇ 2            W     E           ◇ —
    ♣ A J 9 8 7 6 3    S             ♣ 10 5 4 2
                   ♠ A K 9 7 5
                   ♡ K 9
                   ◇ Q 10 8 6 4 3
                   ♣ —
```

SOLUTION 2

North-South vulnerable at IMPs, as South you hold:

♠ 10 9 3 ♡ K 6 ◇ K 10 9 2 ♣ K J 9 4

WEST	NORTH	EAST	SOUTH
		pass	pass
2♠	dbl	3♠	4◇
pass	4♡	pass	?

Bid 5♡. Partner has shown a hand not only too strong to overcall 3♡, but too strong to overcall 4♡, bidding that was intended to be descriptive, not a shutout. With a heart fit, three kings, and good spots, you are easily good enough.

Partner's hand is:

♠ A 4 ♡ A J 7 4 3 2 ◇ A ♣ A Q 5 2

Unfortunately, 7♣ is too hard to find against the opponents' fine defensive bidding.

As an aside, a responsive double would probably have been a better choice than the actual bid of 4◇. A responsive double in my partnerships denies four hearts, and shows the minors. Actually, bidding 4♣ is better than 4◇, but I thought I might get a chance to bid 5♣.

One of my major suggestions for players is to try very hard to describe your hand, if at all possible, instead of cuebidding or making some other nebulous pass-the-buck bid.

To me, 5♡ is a natural, value bid. You have shown values with your 4◇ bid, and now are inviting slam in hearts, showing support for partner's expected long suit and inferentially no spade control. Partner is likely short in spades, but not 100%. Also, partner could cuebid 5♠ (or bid 6♣) on the right hand (this one?), trying for a grand, thus promising first-round spade control.

SOLUTION 3

Neither vulnerable at IMPs, as South you hold:

♠ A K 2 ♡ A 10 ◇ K Q J 9 5 ♣ A 10 5

WEST	NORTH	EAST	SOUTH
1♡	pass	3♡¹	dbl
pass	5♣	pass	?

1. Preemptive.

Bid 6♣. Partner in all likelihood has a singleton heart and a good club suit. You have a hand rich in first-round controls, a source of tricks, and more high cards than partner can expect. And if needed, the East-West hands are pretty much an open book.

You may wonder why you aren't trying for the grand on this deal, but for me, three reasons point towards only six. First, partner may have only the ◇A and ♣KQ32. Also, the 3♡ bid suggests possible bad breaks, and you cannot guard against ♣Jxxx even if partner has five clubs. Finally, partner could have the ◇A and ♣KJxxxx or ♣QJxxxx.

The full deal, from the 2003 CNTC in Penticton:

```
                    ♠ 10 7 5
                    ♡ 2
                    ◇ 10 6
                    ♣ K Q 9 8 4 3 2
  ♠ J 8 4                             ♠ Q 9 6 3
  ♡ K Q J 9 6        N                ♡ 8 7 5 4 3
  ◇ A 8 4 2      W       E            ◇ 7 3
  ♣ 7                S                ♣ J 6
                    ♠ A K 2
                    ♡ A 10
                    ◇ K Q J 9 5
                    ♣ A 10 5
```

SOLUTION 4

Both vulnerable at IMPs, as South you hold:

♠ J 10 8 ♡ A Q 8 4 3 2 ◇ A ♣ A 8 2

WEST	NORTH	EAST	SOUTH
	1NT[1]	pass	2◇[2]
pass	2♡	pass	4◇[3]
dbl	redbl[4]	pass	?

1. 15-17.
2. Transfer.
3. Splinter slam try.
4. Second-round diamond control. Denies a terrible hand for hearts (but it sure is close to that!).

This is an easy one. Bid 5♣. Partner will bid a slam with a spade control (or 5♠ with the ace) and 5♡ without one (**yellow light**).

Partner's hand:

♠ Q 7 ♡ K J ◇ K Q 8 4 ♣ K Q J 9 4

SOLUTION 5

Both vulnerable at IMPs, as South you hold:

♠ Q 10 8 7 6 5 3 ♡ K 5 ◇ 10 7 3 ♣ 8

WEST	NORTH	EAST	SOUTH
1♣	pass	1♡	2♠
3♠	4♠	5♡	?

Pass like a rocket! This is a case of captaincy—and you are not it! You have described your hand reasonably well with your 2♠ vulnerable preempt, with your seventh spade compensating for a poorish suit and minimal high cards.

> *The difference between genius*
> *and stupidity is that*
> *genius has its limits.*
> *– Author unknown*

The full deal:

```
                    ♠ K J 9 4 2
                    ♡ 9 7
                    ◇ K 9 2
                    ♣ K Q 9
   ♠ —                            ♠ A
   ♡ Q 8 3 2        N             ♡ A J 10 6 4
   ◇ A J 4      W       E         ◇ Q 8 6 5
   ♣ A J 7 6 5 2     S            ♣ 10 4 3
                    ♠ Q 10 8 7 6 5 3
                    ♡ K 5
                    ◇ 10 7 3
                    ♣ 8
```

The South player at the table not only broke captaincy, but also demonstrated poor judgment, in my opinion, by bidding 5♠. Probably he felt the 2♠ call had not sufficiently described his hand.

> **Tip 27** The opponents are not infallible. Don't rely on them to have the perfect hand for their bids, especially when they are under pressure, as in the above deal.

SOLUTION 6

East-West vulnerable at matchpoints, as South you hold:

♠ A ♡ Q 7 5 2 ◇ A ♣ A Q J 10 7 4 2

WEST	NORTH	EAST	SOUTH
2♡	3◇	3♡	?

Bid 6♣. There is no science that will enable you to solicit information from partner. Bidding 4♣ might work, but partner may get overly excited with first-round heart control, no ♣K, and non-solid diamonds, say:

♠ K Q 10 ♡ A ◇ K J 10 9 8 7 6 5 ♣ 5

After you make a value call, partner might even be able to go to 7♣ with the first round of hearts controlled and the ♣K. Cuebidding would confuse the issue, and partner might play you for diamond support. In fact, bidding 6♣ would have scored you 11 out of 12 matchpoints.

The full deal:

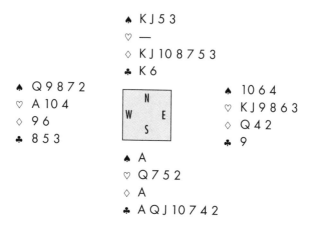

```
                    ♠ K J 5 3
                    ♡ —
                    ◊ K J 10 8 7 5 3
                    ♣ K 6
 ♠ Q 9 8 7 2                         ♠ 10 6 4
 ♡ A 10 4          N                 ♡ K J 9 8 6 3
 ◊ 9 6        W         E            ◊ Q 4 2
 ♣ 8 5 3          S                  ♣ 9
                    ♠ A
                    ♡ Q 7 5 2
                    ◊ A
                    ♣ A Q J 10 7 4 2
```

SOLUTION 7

East-West vulnerable at matchpoints, as South you hold:

♠ Q 8 3   ♡ K Q 7 2   ◊ 8 3   ♣ A 10 8 3

WEST	NORTH	EAST	SOUTH
	pass	pass	1♣
1◊	1♠	pass	pass
2◊	dbl	3♣	?

Double! Yes, you do not have an opening bid. However, partner has made a penalty double of 2◊. If North had hearts, longer spades or club support, he would just bid the appropriate suit. He has already shown spades.

You have the other two suits and reasonable defense. How do you know partner has a good hand? Because he doubled *knowing* you did not have a full opening bid after your pass of 1♠. If you trust partner, double. The full deal:

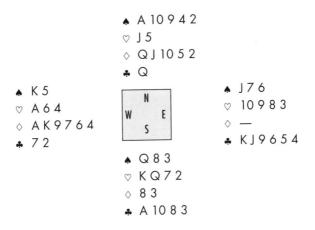

♠ A 10 9 4 2
♡ J 5
◇ Q J 10 5 2
♣ Q

♠ K 5
♡ A 6 4
◇ A K 9 7 6 4
♣ 7 2

♠ J 7 6
♡ 10 9 8 3
◇ —
♣ K J 9 6 5 4

♠ Q 8 3
♡ K Q 7 2
◇ 8 3
♣ A 10 8 3

SOLUTION 8

Both vulnerable at IMPs, as South you hold:

♠ A ♡ K 10 9 6 4 ◇ 4 ♣ A K Q 9 7 5

WEST	NORTH	EAST	SOUTH
		1◇	?

The choices are: double, 2♣, 1♡ and 2NT. Don't bid 2NT, showing the two lowest unbid suits; the disadvantage of this call is that your suits are very different in length and quality. Overcalling 1♡ is just wrong—you would never be able to convince your partner you have more than five clubs. Double is possible, as you do have a very strong hand, with only three losers.

However, I would recommend 2♣. There is little danger of the bidding dying, especially since East will usually reopen in case partner has a penalty double of 2♣. Whatever happens, you will bid your hearts, probably at the three-level considering there is a negative double on your left. In order to force partner to the four- or five-level, you must have a hand something like this.

A likely auction:

WEST	NORTH	EAST	SOUTH
		1◇	2♣
dbl[1]	pass	2♠	3♡

1. Negative.

SOLUTION 9

North-South vulnerable at matchpoints, as North you hold:

♠ J 8 4 3 ♡ 10 7 5 ◇ A J 5 2 ♣ K 7

WEST	NORTH	EAST	SOUTH
pass	pass	1♡	1♠
pass	2♡¹	3♡	pass
pass	?		

1. Limit raise in spades.

Pass. You have already shown your hand, so trust partner has made the right decision and pass. Partner could have bid three spades competitively if he had wanted to do that opposite a limit raise. He didn't. Your heart holding and heart bidding is ominous.

At the 2004 Atlanta Regional, my partner bid 3♠ and we were doubled. Not surprisingly, West had a singleton heart and got a ruff, so I went down two for –500. I actually had a pretty good overcall:

♠ K Q 10 9 5 ♡ K Q ◇ 6 4 3 ♣ Q J 5

SOLUTION 10

Both vulnerable at IMPs, as North you hold:

♠ K 4 2 ♡ J 10 8 7 2 ◇ Q 7 ♣ 10 9 5

WEST	NORTH	EAST	SOUTH
pass	pass	1♣	dbl
pass	1♡	pass	2♣
pass	?		

Bid 3♡. Your one heart was forced, and it shows 0-8 points. Partner has forced you to bid, showing a good hand. You definitely have close to a maximum, especially with a fifth heart and good intermediates.

> *When I take a 50-50 chance, I expect it*
> *to come off 8 or 9 times out of 10.*
> – Victor Mollo's 'Hideous Hog'

The full deal, from the 2005 CNTC:

```
                    ♠ K 4 2
                    ♡ J 10 8 7 2
                    ◇ Q 7
                    ♣ 10 9 5
    ♠ 10 9 3           ┌─────────┐        ♠ J 7 6 5
    ♡ 6 4 3            │    N    │        ♡ K
    ◇ J 6 2            │  W   E  │        ◇ 9 4 3
    ♣ J 7 6 3          │    S    │        ♣ A K Q 8 4
                       └─────────┘
                    ♠ A Q 8
                    ♡ A Q 9 5
                    ◇ A K 10 8 5
                    ♣ 2
```

Partner will likely just bid 6♡, knowing that major-suit finesses will be onside.

SOLUTION 11

North-South vulnerable at IMPs, as South you hold:

♠ 6 ♡ J 4 ◇ A K Q J 10 6 4 ♣ J 9 4

WEST	NORTH	EAST	SOUTH
		pass	?

I think 3◇ is the right call. If you open 1◇, partner is likely to play you for more defense and/or convertible values. By bidding 3◇ you:

a) Show the essence of your hand;
b) Take away valuable bidding space from the opponents; *and*
c) Let partner take control with the knowledge that your hand is close to what he should expect.

Obviously, this is a partnership agreement issue. But I would recommend for any partnership that a vulnerable against not preempt in first or second seat should show a very good suit. The other way many partnerships describe this hand is with a gambling 3NT opening. The main problem with this approach is that you wrong-side 3NT, as the lead is coming through your partner's stoppers.

At the 2006 World Bridge Championships, both Vilas Boas and Henner-Welland, playing for Chagas and Henner-Welland respectively, opened 1◇ and wound up at the five-level going for −1100 and −800, instead of a quiet −450.

SOLUTION 12

Both vulnerable at IMPs, as South you hold:

♠ A K 9 7 4 ♡ A K 2 ◇ K 2 ♣ Q J 2

WEST	NORTH	EAST	SOUTH
	pass	1♠	pass
1NT	pass	2♣	pass
2◇	pass	pass	?

Pass. Where are you going? Partner has roughly zero points, maybe two on a good day. If you declare, there will likely be no entry to dummy. How many tricks can you take in 2NT? My guess is five. Why go for −800?

In the 2003 CNTC, Rick Delogu passed and 2◇ made three. The full deal:

```
                    ♠ J 10
                    ♡ J 10 9
                    ◇ 8 5 4
                    ♣ 9 8 6 5 4
  ♠ 8                                ♠ Q 6 5 3 2
  ♡ 8 5 4 3          N               ♡ Q 7 6
  ◇ A Q 10 9 7 6   W   E             ◇ J 3
  ♣ 10 3             S               ♣ A K 7
                    ♠ A K 9 7 4
                    ♡ A K 2
                    ◇ K 2
                    ♣ Q J 2
```

Despite partner having a great hand, you probably go down two for −500 in 2NT doubled.

> **Tip 28** You can't win events on every deal. Don't take unnecessary or high risks.

SOLUTION 13

Both vulnerable at IMPs, as South you hold:

♠ A 6 ♡ K 9 ◇ A K 8 7 6 2 ♣ A J 8

WEST	NORTH	EAST	SOUTH
	3♠	pass	?

Either sign off in 6♠, or try Keycard Blackwood looking for seven.

Obviously, it is important to know what type of preempts you and your partner play, but with a normal partnership you have enough values for slam. Two of the key issues to consider are vulnerability and seat. A third-seat not vulnerable versus vulnerable preempt can be very undisciplined (in most partnerships) compared to the actual situation—partner opening vulnerable, in first seat. Partner's hand:

♠ K J 9 8 5 4 3 2 ♡ J ◇ J 3 ♣ Q 6

SOLUTION 14

East-West vulnerable at matchpoints, as South you hold:

♠ K 9 7 6 ♡ A 9 8 5 4 3 ◇ 10 ♣ 5 2

WEST	NORTH	EAST	SOUTH
pass	pass	1◇	1♡
pass	pass	dbl	pass
1NT	pass	pass	?

Pass. The full deal:

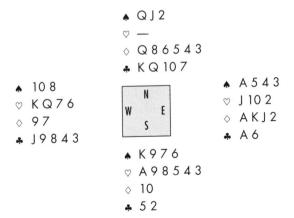

```
                    ♠ Q J 2
                    ♡ —
                    ◇ Q 8 6 5 4 3
                    ♣ K Q 10 7
    ♠ 10 8                          ♠ A 5 4 3
    ♡ K Q 7 6        N              ♡ J 10 2
    ◇ 9 7       W         E         ◇ A K J 2
    ♣ J 9 8 4 3       S             ♣ A 6
                    ♠ K 9 7 6
                    ♡ A 9 8 5 4 3
                    ◇ 10
                    ♣ 5 2
```

The player at the table thought as he was not vulnerable he would push the opponents higher, out of 1NT. He bid 2♡, got doubled and went down three, -500. His hand is an overcall, barely. It is worth one call. He had a partner—but didn't trust him!

SOLUTION 15

Both vulnerable at IMPs, as South you hold:

♠ K 7 ♡ A Q 7 ◇ A 8 6 4 ♣ A 8 5 2

WEST	NORTH	EAST	SOUTH
1♠	pass	2♠	dbl
pass	4♡	4♠	?

Double. You have a fairly clear preference for defending—only three hearts, and a doubleton spade (you could have had only one and good defense).

At the table, South passed and heard partner bid 5♡. This was doubled, down three. The full deal:

```
              ♠ 2
              ♡ 9 6 4 3 2
              ◇ K Q J 2
              ♣ J 9 3
♠ A Q 10 9 8        ┌───────┐        ♠ J 6 5 4 3
♡ K 10 8 5          │   N   │        ♡ J
◇ 9 7              │ W   E │        ◇ 10 5 3
♣ Q 6              │   S   │        ♣ K 10 7 4
                   └───────┘
              ♠ K 7
              ♡ A Q 7
              ◇ A 8 6 4
              ♣ A 8 5 2
```

It is worth discussing this auction with your partner and deciding whether a pass by South is forcing. For me it would be: you are vulnerable, bid voluntarily to game, and the player who started with a limited 2♠ bid is obviously sacrificing.

SOLUTION 16

Both vulnerable at IMPs, as North you hold:

♠ 9 6 5 2 ♡ Q 8 6 2 ◇ A 7 6 2 ♣ 3

WEST	NORTH	EAST	SOUTH
pass	pass	2◇ 1	3◇
4◇	dbl	4♡	pass
pass	?		

1. 11-15 HCP, three-suiter short in diamonds (could be 3-4 or 4-3 in majors).

The actual North player in this situation was Zia Mahmood, one of the best bridge players alive today, and a man who arguably has the best table presence and judgment at the bridge table. Despite that, I disagree with his 5◇ bid. I think the correct call is double. First, partner will have sound values bidding vulnerable, and obviously a good suit. He also passed over 4♡, suggesting he doesn't have a strong opinion of bidding more. West, a passed hand, is forcing to game with both majors and likely diamond shortage. But he is under great pressure. Where are the clubs? The most likely split is five with East, four with partner and three with West.

In summary, I think it's likely that declarer will have some club losers, and will not be able to handle diamond leads at every opportunity.

The full deal:

Zia
♠ 9 6 5 2
♡ Q 8 6 2
◇ A 7 6 2
♣ 3

Geoff Hampson
♠ J 10 8 3
♡ A J 9 3
◇ J 4
♣ Q 8 7

```
      N
  W       E
      S
```

Eric Greco
♠ A 7 4
♡ K 7 5 4
◇ Q
♣ K 10 9 5 2

Michael Rosenberg
♠ K Q
♡ 10
◇ K 10 9 8 5 3
♣ A J 6 4

In the 2005 US Team Trials to determine the second team to play in the Bermuda Bowl, Welland lost a big opportunity for a 12-IMP or greater swing when 5◇ went down one doubled for –200, while 4♡ doubled would have been down at least two for +500.

SOLUTION 17

North-South vulnerable at matchpoints, as South you hold:

♠ K 9 6 5   ♡ J 10 7 3 2   ◇ 6 4   ♣ K 8

WEST	NORTH	EAST	SOUTH
		pass	pass
1♡	2♣	2♡	?

Double or bid on? Jeff Meckstroth, arguably one of two or three top players in the world today, bid 3♣ in the 2003 European Pairs Championships. Top-class declarer play by his partner and peer Eric Rodwell allowed them to score +110 in 3♣ along the way to winning this prestigious event. What about 2♡ doubled you might ask?

The full deal:

```
                    Rodwell
                    ♠ 10 2
                    ♡ 8
                    ◇ A Q 10 8
                    ♣ A Q J 10 4 3
     ♠ A Q J 8                          ♠ 7 4 3
     ♡ A 9 5 4        N                 ♡ K Q 6
     ◇ J 7 5 2     W     E              ◇ K 9 3
     ♣ 6              S                 ♣ 9 7 5 2
                    Meckstroth
                    ♠ K 9 6 5
                    ♡ J 10 7 3 2
                    ◇ 6 4
                    ♣ K 8
```

On any reasonable expert line of play, 2♡ is cold and may easily make an overtrick. Bidding on by South is indicated at matchpoints, as (1) you may only collect +100 and be cold for +110 and (2) you may push the opponents to 3♡, which I would double.

SOLUTION 18

Both vulnerable at IMPs, as West you hold:

♠ Q 6 2 ♡ K 9 7 3 ◇ A K 3 ♣ 4 3 2

WEST	NORTH	EAST	SOUTH
			1♠
pass	2♠¹	pass	pass
?			

1. Weak two-level raise.

Pass. Sure, North may be weak, but South might have a decent hand and have passed knowing no game has a chance. In that scenario, he's hoping you balance. That is exactly what turned out to be the case at the 2003 US Team Trials.

The full deal:

Fallenius
♠ 8 7 4
♡ J 6 5 2
◇ 10 2
♣ A Q 7 5

Wolff
♠ Q 6 2
♡ K 9 7 3
◇ A K 3
♣ 4 3 2

```
      N
   W     E
      S
```

Morse
♠ 10 3
♡ Q 10 8
◇ Q J 8 5
♣ J 10 9 6

Welland
♠ A K J 9 5
♡ A 4
◇ 9 7 6 4
♣ K 8

Bobby Wolff balanced with a double. His partner, Dan Morse, bid 3♣, and that went down three. The story has a twist in the tail, as Bjorn Fallenius with the North hand didn't double 3♣ for some reason (he couldn't have had a better hand in his partnership system). So he and Welland were only +300 instead of +800, winning 4 IMPs instead of 12 IMPs (North-South were +170 in 3♠ at the other table).

SOLUTION 19

Both vulnerable at IMPs, as South you hold:

♠ Q 9 6 4 3 ♡ A K 7 4 3 ◇ K Q 8 ♣ —

WEST	NORTH	EAST	SOUTH
pass	1◇	pass	1♠
pass	2◇	pass	2♡
pass	2♠	pass	?

The key point of the bidding has arrived—if this weren't a problem, would you be ready? The question your next bid will answer is, 'Which suit will be trumps?'

The answer to that is surely diamonds, so bid 3◇ now, setting the trump suit. Partner likely has at least six diamonds and exactly three spades. Your spades are weak. If you have one or more spade losers, they may go away on the heart suit, when diamonds are trumps. This can't happen in spades.

Partner actually held:

♠ A 7 5 ♡ 9 6 ◇ A J 9 7 6 5 ♣ K 2

So 6◇ made, but 6♠ went down on a mildly bad spade distribution.

SOLUTION 20

Both vulnerable at IMPs, as South you hold:

♠ J 5 4 3 ♡ Q 9 5 ◇ A 6 ♣ A K 8 6

WEST	NORTH	EAST	SOUTH
1◇	pass	pass	dbl
pass	1♠	pass	?

Bid 2♠. A balancing double can be made with as little as 8-9 HCP, as long as the hand is short in opener's suit. Even though partner did not overcall 1♠, he may still have a decent hand with a four-card spade suit. A 2♠ raise here says, 'I have a decent double—around a good opening bid—and spade support'. With another ace or king you would bid 3♠.

SOLUTION 21

East-West vulnerable at IMPs, as South you hold:

♠ A K Q 8 4 3 2 ♡ A Q ◇ 4 2 ♣ 9 6

WEST	NORTH	EAST	SOUTH
1♡	pass	1NT	?

Pass! Why bid? If 1NT gets passed out, you can beat it three tricks for sure, and probably one or two more than that, which is as much as your non-vulnerable game is worth. This can work only if you do it in tempo, of course.

But at the table at the 2004 CNTC, this story had an unhappy ending. I passed in tempo and the bidding continued 3♡, pass, 3NT. I was licking my lips! However, Joey Silver, sitting on my left, must have detected some saliva on me, as he bid 4♡ now. This came back to me and I bid 4♠, which went one down. Oh well, I tried.

As it turned out, it would probably have worked out better to make the 'picture' bid of 4♠, but then I would have given up the chance of defending 3NT—and I couldn't resist that!

SOLUTION 22

Neither vulnerable at IMPs, as South you hold:

♠ — ♡ Q 7 2 ◇ A Q 10 9 6 5 4 ♣ A 8 4

WEST	NORTH	EAST	SOUTH
1♠	3♡¹	4♠	?

1. Preemptive.

This is a great hand, but difficult to judge and bid. You don't know who can make what, and at what level. If partner fits diamonds, both sides can make a lot of tricks. However, if partner is void in diamonds, they probably are going down in 4♠.

I think the best bid is 5◇. Although 5♡ may work better, I prefer 5◇ for three reasons. First, if they double, you can convert to 5♡, painting a nice picture of your hand, and partner should be able to make the right decision. If they bid 5♠ over 5♡, partner can bid on with a diamond fit. Secondly, you have indicated what suit you want partner to lead against any spade contract. Finally, hearts may have some play issues against a 3-1 or 4-0 heart split, especially when he has three or four spades. However, bidding 5♡ directly will probably work better if they bid 5♠, as then you can bid 6◇, which I think shows this type of strength and distribution.

You may not always be right, but an important principle behind this type of decision is to try and visualize how your bid will work, with the likely subsequent bidding.

SOLUTION 23

Neither vulnerable at IMPs, as South you hold:

♠ Q ♡ K J 6 ◇ A Q 10 5 4 3 ♣ A Q J

WEST	NORTH	EAST	SOUTH
pass	pass	2♡	?

What do you bid? This is a hand where nothing is really appetizing. You are too strong for 3◇, while a double will possibly get you 4♠. I chose to bid 3NT. A key factor for me is the second heart stopper. If LHO doubles, I will run to 4◇, which should give partner some idea of what I have.

The full deal:

```
                ♠ A 3 2
                ♡ 7 2
                ◇ J 7 2
                ♣ K 7 5 4 2
  ♠ K 8 7 6 4                    ♠ J 10 9 5
  ♡ A 8            N              ♡ Q 10 9 5 4 3
  ◇ K 9 6      W       E          ◇ 8
  ♣ 10 8 3         S              ♣ 9 6
                ♠ Q
                ♡ K J 6
                ◇ A Q 10 5 4 3
                ♣ A Q J
```

They did not find the ♠K lead and I made five.

SOLUTION 24

Both vulnerable at IMPs, as South you hold:

♠ K J 10 2   ♡ Q J 7   ◇ A 7 4 3 2   ♣ 6

WEST	NORTH	EAST	SOUTH
			1◇
pass	1♡	pass	?

Bid 2♡. Why? Your hand is worth only one more bid, and this is the most constructive call you can make. If partner has a good hand with spades, he will bid them. Occasionally you will play in a 4-3 instead of 4-4 when partner has both majors. But sometimes...

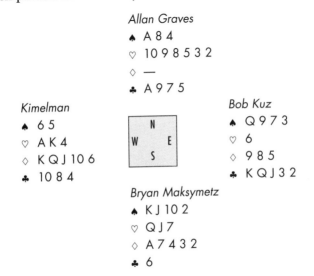

Allan Graves
♠ A 8 4
♡ 10 9 8 5 3 2
◇ —
♣ A 9 7 5

Kimelman
♠ 6 5
♡ A K 4
◇ K Q J 10 6
♣ 10 8 4

Bob Kuz
♠ Q 9 7 3
♡ 6
◇ 9 8 5
♣ K Q J 3 2

Bryan Maksymetz
♠ K J 10 2
♡ Q J 7
◇ A 7 4 3 2
♣ 6

Bryan Maksymetz, one of the most successful Canadian players in international competition, bid 1♠ in the 2003 CNTC and it went all pass! Meanwhile, 4♡ is unbeatable, and that's what North would have bid over 2♡. Bryan, showing a lot of class and interest in maintaining partnership harmony, apologized to his partner for bidding too quickly as Graves was putting down the dummy.

SOLUTION 25

Neither vulnerable at IMPs, as South you hold:

♠ 5 ♡ 4 2 ◇ A Q 9 ♣ A K Q 10 9 8 3

WEST	NORTH	EAST	SOUTH
			1♣
2♡	2♠	4♡	5♣
pass	5♠	pass	?

Trust partner and pass. You have shown an excellent, if not solid, club suit. Partner has returned to his own suit, showing a solid suit. Why else would he bid? What about slam—is that a possibility? Again, if you trust partner, he does not have a heart control, or he would have bid either 6♠ or 5♡.

This hand occurred in the 1987 Spingold final. Michael Seamon inexplicably bid 6♣ over his partner's 5♠ bid.

Partner (Roy Fox) held:

♠ A K Q J 10 8 7 4 ♡ J 3 ◇ 7 5 ♣ 2

SOLUTION 26

North-South vulnerable at matchpoints, as South you hold:

♠ 9 7 ♡ A K Q 10 9 8 7 5 4 ◇ — ♣ J 5

WEST	NORTH	EAST	SOUTH
pass	1◇	pass	1♡
pass	2♣	pass	?

This hand came up recently at a local game. Although you may get too high, I think the best call is 5♡. This gets across to partner the facts that you are interested in slam, have a self-sufficient suit and are looking for aces and a spade control for slam. Going slow does not get across this message with any type of certainty.

Another option is to shoot out 6♡, giving the opponents a blind lead. I think 5♡ accomplishes the same thing, as with a reasonable hand with good controls partner will go on to 6♡, leaving the same guess on lead. The other advantage of 5♡ is that partner may be interested in a grand slam, with, for example:

♠ A 7 5 ♡ 3 ◇ K 8 7 6 5 ♣ A K Q 10

SOLUTION 27

Neither vulnerable at IMPs, as South you hold:

♠ A 10 9 8 6   ♡ 8   ◇ Q 5 2   ♣ J 8 5 2

WEST	NORTH	EAST	SOUTH
			pass
pass	pass	1♡	1♠
2♣	2♡	pass	2♠
3♡	3♠	4♡	pass
pass	dbl	pass	?

Pass. You have your values for a 1♠ overcall, although you are minimum. You showed a minimum over your partner's 2♡ and 3♠ bids. Now he's doubled them. What's the problem? Trust partner.

As you may suspect, this hand had an unhappy ending at the table. During the 1987 Spingold final, Tom Mahaffey bid 4♠ here. He deservedly went down three doubled for -500, when 4♡ was down one in top tricks. Partner had:

♠ J 7 3   ♡ K Q J 4   ◇ J 9 8 3   ◇ A 9

SOLUTION 28

North-South vulnerable at IMPs, as South you hold:

♠ 3 2   ♡ 7 6 5   ◇ Q 9 5 3 2   ♣ A Q 7

WEST	NORTH	EAST	SOUTH
1♡	dbl	4♡	?

Bid 5◇. Partner is marked with at most one heart, so must have good support for the unbid suits. There is no guarantee, but my experience has shown that often in this type of situation both games will make. That is exactly what happened to Roger Bates at the 2006 World Championships! He passed, and the full deal was:

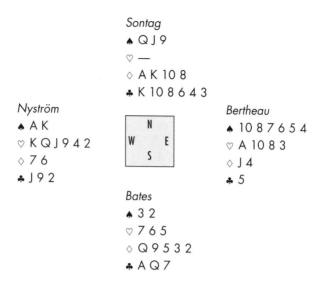

Sontag
♠ Q J 9
♡ —
◇ A K 10 8
♣ K 10 8 6 4 3

Nyström
♠ A K
♡ K Q J 9 4 2
◇ 7 6
♣ J 9 2

Bertheau
♠ 10 8 7 6 5 4
♡ A 10 8 3
◇ J 4
♣ 5

Bates
♠ 3 2
♡ 7 6 5
◇ Q 9 5 3 2
♣ A Q 7

SOLUTION 29

East-West vulnerable at IMPs, as South you hold:

♠ 10 8 3 2   ♡ 9 8   ◇ 8 5 3   ♣ A Q J 10

WEST	NORTH	EAST	SOUTH
			pass
pass	1 ♠	pass	2 ♠
pass	3 ◇	pass	3 ♠
pass	4 ♣	pass	?

Bid 5♣. Your hand is a minimum in terms of high cards. However, you have four spades and two of the top three honors in the suit that partner has bid.

Partner's hand was:

♠ A K J 7 6 5 4   ♡ —   ◇ A Q 5   ♣ K 9 4

As you can see, partner needs no further encouraging. If the ◇Q were the ◇K, partner would be at minimum looking for 7♠, and maybe just bidding it. Incidentally, if your clubs were AQJ62, the best call would be 6♣, announcing very good club values in a longer suit.

SOLUTION 30

North-South vulnerable at IMPs, as South you hold:

♠ A 10 9 8 6 2   ♡ 8   ♢ K J 9 7   ♣ K Q

WEST	NORTH	EAST	SOUTH
1♢	1♠	dbl	4♠
5♢	5♠	pass	?

This hand is from the 2005 Bermuda Bowl. Representing Canada were George Mittelman, who held the South hand, and Arno Hobart (North). Instead of automatically passing 5♠, as would be normal on this type of auction, Mittelman asked himself, 'What can partner have for his 5♠ bid?'

He concluded that, besides at least five spades, partner must have a diamond void and an ace. He therefore bid 6♠, which should be cold or close to it opposite the envisioned North hand.

Hobart's actual hand was:

♠ K Q J 4 3   ♡ A 7 4 3   ♢ —   ♣ 10 8 3 2

Bidding 6♠ gained a well-deserved slam swing.

> *Card sense is when it's technically right*
> *to do something, and the little man that sits*
> *on my shoulder or anyone else's shoulder*
> *says, "Don't do that." And you say to*
> *yourself, "Well, wait a minute, that's*
> *the right way to play." And he says,*
> *"Yeah, but you don't wanna play that way."*
>
> *That instinct is card sense. It's almost*
> *an ability to feel where the cards are.*
> *It's something that you can't buy, you*
> *can't find; you're born with it. The*
> *ability to do the right thing at the*
> *wrong time or really to do the wrong*
> *thing at the right time.*
> — Barry Crane

SOLUTION 31

Neither vulnerable at IMPs, as South you hold:

♠ K Q 9 3 2 ♡ A Q J 9 8 4 3 ◇ — ♣ 8

WEST	NORTH	EAST	SOUTH
	pass	pass	1♡
2NT	pass	3◇	3♠
5◇	dbl	pass	?

Pass. South has done a very good job describing his hand. Opposite a passed hand he has forced to the four-level, so partner knows South has a lot of playing strength. The full deal:

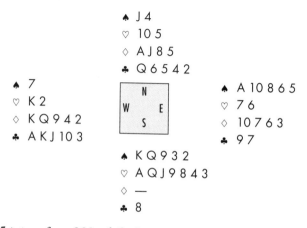

          ♠ J 4
          ♡ 10 5
          ◇ A J 8 5
          ♣ Q 6 5 4 2

♠ 7   ♠ A 10 8 6 5
♡ K 2   ♡ 7 6
◇ K Q 9 4 2   ◇ 10 7 6 3
♣ A K J 10 3   ♣ 9 7

          ♠ K Q 9 3 2
          ♡ A Q J 9 8 4 3
          ◇ —
          ♣ 8

We beat 5◇ two for +300 while 5♡ went down two at the other table.

SOLUTION 32

North-South vulnerable at IMPs, as South you hold:

♠ A J ♡ A 2 ◇ K Q 10 7 6 5 ♣ A 9 7

WEST	NORTH	EAST	SOUTH
	pass	1♠	dbl
4♠	5♡	dbl	?

I think the best call is 6◇. I also think it is right to bid 6◇ if RHO passes instead of doubling. Your plan was to double and bid diamonds to show a hand too strong for an immediate 2◇ overcall. Stick to the plan! You have not yet described your hand. Partner is expecting you to have at least three hearts. The double is ominous.

This hand is from the 2006 World Bridge Championships in Verona, Italy. The full deal:

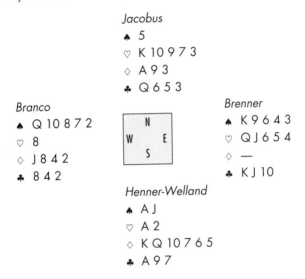

Jacobus
- ♠ 5
- ♡ K 10 9 7 3
- ◇ A 9 3
- ♣ Q 6 5 3

Branco
- ♠ Q 10 8 7 2
- ♡ 8
- ◇ J 8 4 2
- ♣ 8 4 2

Brenner
- ♠ K 9 6 4 3
- ♡ Q J 6 5 4
- ◇ —
- ♣ K J 10

Henner-Welland
- ♠ A J
- ♡ A 2
- ◇ K Q 10 7 6 5
- ♣ A 9 7

Henner-Welland passed on this auction and was –800 in 5♡ doubled. It turns out 6◇ is also down one or two on this layout. However, if you switch the ♣K and the ♣Q, 6◇ is a much better contract than 5♡.

Earlier in this book, I discussed the pros and cons of doubling and overcalling. This deal is a good example. Although you definitely have a very strong overcall, your partnership would be better placed over the 4♠ bid had you initially bid 2◇ instead of doubling.

SOLUTION 33
Neither vulnerable at IMPs, as South you hold:

♠ 3 2 ♡ 9 ◇ A Q 9 8 ♣ Q 10 9 8 7 2

WEST	NORTH	EAST	SOUTH
	1♡	1NT	?

I bid 3♣, which I thought was creative. I knew I wouldn't be doubled, and in case they had a spade fit, I wanted to force them to act at the three-level. The other advantage of 3♣ is that partner may have a good hand with club support, and we may have a game. I made a call that described my playing strength, so that partner could act intelligently. I could also double any further bidding by the opponents, showing a strong playing hand for clubs with not quite enough HCP to double 1NT. Then I could comfortably abide by partner's decision to pass or pull. The full deal from the 2005 CNTC:

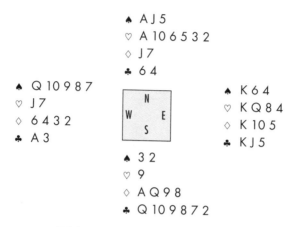

As you can see, 1NT would have made on a club lead if declarer attacked hearts. Meanwhile, 3♣ made, despite partner's 'minimum'. Switch the ♡2 for the ♣A and 5♣ is cold, and the bidding would have started out the same!

> *I think we are all a bit*
> *masochistic. Otherwise, why would*
> *we continue to play bridge?*
> – Author unknown

SOLUTION 34

Both vulnerable at IMPs, as South you hold:

♠ 6 5   ♡ A J 10 9 3   ◇ K 10   ♣ A Q 10 5

WEST	NORTH	EAST	SOUTH
pass	pass	1♡	pass
1♠	pass	pass	dbl
pass	1NT	pass	?

Bid 3NT. What does partner have? Yes, a spade stopper and some values, but he does not need to be strong as he knows you have a heart trap pass. Repeating a point I made earlier, I think most bridge players undervalue the great advantage to declarer of having heard an opponent open the bidding. You can often make game with less than the normal 25-26 HCP as you are playing close to double dummy. Besides possibly having to give a trick away on the opening lead, the opener is almost always subject to squeezes or endplays in the course of the play.

The full deal, in which Wang for China bid 2NT and played it there, from the 2005 Venice Cup match between China and England:

```
                        Liu
                        ♠ K Q 9 7
                        ♡ 7 4
                        ◇ Q J 8 7
                        ♣ 8 7 6
  Dhondy                                    Smith
  ♠ A 8 3 2          ┌─────────┐            ♠ J 10 4
  ♡ K               │    N    │            ♡ Q 8 6 5 2
  ◇ 9 6 5 3         │  W   E  │            ◇ A 4 2
  ♣ 9 4 3 2         │    S    │            ♣ K J
                     └─────────┘
                        Wang
                        ♠ 6 5
                        ♡ A J 10 9 3
                        ◇ K 10
                        ♣ A Q 10 5
```

SOLUTION 35

North-South vulnerable at IMPs, as South you hold:

♠ A Q 10 3 2   ♡ A K J   ◇ —   ♣ A Q 8 6 2

WEST	NORTH	EAST	SOUTH
pass	pass	4◇	?

Tough hand! I bid 5◇ —and over partner's 5♡ bid, I bid 5♠ to show clubs and spades, with a strong hand (indeed, a hand better than my actual one). My philosophy on hands like this is to find the best trump suit, even if I have to risk the wrong level. Bidding 5◇ is aggressive compared to 4NT and double. The advantage of the other two options is that partner may bid hearts, but even then you have no idea whether hearts will play well. Indeed, you can visualize communication problems and having to ruff diamonds with high heart honors. My thinking was that 5◇ will focus on two suits instead of one, and I can show my diamond control/big hand along the way. Partner saved us by having the right stuff and we played in 6♣:

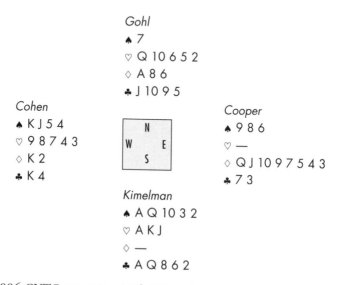

Gohl
♠ 7
♡ Q 10 6 5 2
◇ A 8 6
♣ J 10 9 5

Cohen
♠ K J 5 4
♡ 9 8 7 4 3
◇ K 2
♣ K 4

Cooper
♠ 9 8 6
♡ —
◇ Q J 10 9 7 5 4 3
♣ 7 3

Kimelman
♠ A Q 10 3 2
♡ A K J
◇ —
♣ A Q 8 6 2

At the 2006 CNTC, we gained 16 IMPs when the opponent who held my cards at the other table did not bid 5◇, and they eventually played in an unmakable 6♡.

SOLUTION 36

East-West vulnerable at IMPs, as South you hold:

♠ Q 6 5 3 2 ♡ K 7 ◇ 7 ♣ 9 7 4 3 2

WEST	NORTH	EAST	SOUTH
	1♣	1◇	1♠
2♣	pass	2♡	?

Bid 3♣. I thought you could use an easy one. Although it wasn't so easy for Argentina's rising star Agustin Madala, who passed as South, scored up –620, and lost 11 IMPs at the 2005 World Championships. At the other table, North-South found their good 5♣ sacrifice, for –100.

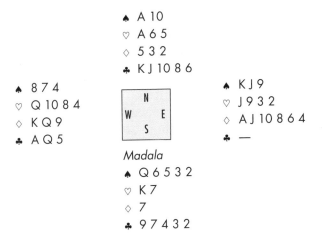

♠ A 10
♡ A 6 5
◇ 5 3 2
♣ K J 10 8 6

♠ 8 7 4
♡ Q 10 8 4
◇ K Q 9
♣ A Q 5

♠ K J 9
♡ J 9 3 2
◇ A J 10 8 6 4
♣ —

Madala
♠ Q 6 5 3 2
♡ K 7
◇ 7
♣ 9 7 4 3 2

SOLUTION 37

Neither vulnerable at IMPs, as South you hold:

♠ A K Q 8 4 ♡ 10 5 ◇ J 8 3 ♣ A Q 4

WEST	NORTH	EAST	SOUTH
	1◇	pass	1♠
pass	2◇	pass	3♣
pass	3♡	pass	3NT
pass	4♠	pass	?

First, let us try and understand what partner has. The 2◇ rebid usually shows at least six diamonds. Your 3♣ created a virtual game force, showing a club suit or club values. Partner bid 3♡. One thing partner does not have is an average minimum with five diamonds and four hearts, or even six diamonds and four hearts, as with these hands he would simply bid 3NT.

No, he is either showing a very distributional hand, or more likely, a good hand. Your 3NT is questionable given the above information, and 4◇ would have been a better call, showing a '**green light**' with your diamond fit and extra values. The only problem is that there may be some wastage opposite a red two-suiter.

Now 4♠ paints a pretty good picture of partner's hand: he has three-card spade support, short clubs and a good hand. Therefore, I think that 4NT is probably best now. A case could be made for 4NT here being for play—another agreement a partnership needs to decide on. However, from my perspective, 4NT logically should not be natural, as the only hand possible for South is 4-3-2-4, with no heart stopper. With that holding you have to play in either 4♠ or 5◇, leaving 4NT for all hands on which you want to ask for keycards. If partner shows two keycards, then 5NT invites a grand slam, in case partner has solid diamonds. On the actual hand, partner will bid 6♡, showing two kings. You will sign off in 6♠.

The two hands:

```
            ♠ 9 7 3
            ♡ A K 2
            ◇ A K 10 7 6 2
            ♣ 9

                 N
            W         E
                 S

            ♠ A K Q 8 4
            ♡ 10 5
            ◇ J 8 3
            ♣ A Q 4
```

> *Posse quam possunt.*
> *(They can because they*
> *think they can.)*
> – Virgil

SOLUTION 38

East-West vulnerable at IMPs, as South you hold:

♠ A Q 3 ♡ J 10 9 6 5 ◇ K 10 4 ♣ A Q

WEST	NORTH	EAST	SOUTH
		2♠	?

Bid 2NT. This is a better description of your hand than 3♡. You have two spade stoppers and a poorish five-card heart suit. The full deal:

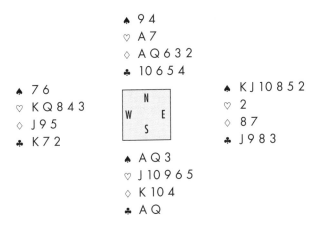

As you can see, 3NT makes easily where 4♡ may go down if declarer tries to ruff a spade.

SOLUTION 39

East-West vulnerable at IMPs, as South you hold:

♠ A K 4   ♡ A K 9 5   ◇ 8 4   ♣ 9 7 6 2

WEST	NORTH	EAST	SOUTH
		1◇	1♡[1]
pass	4◇[2]	dbl	4♠
pass	5♣	dbl	?

1. Double is a better bid, but I was trying to do something a little different.
2. Splinter.

Bid 5♡. It looks like you created some action, but is it good action? This auction is a classic case of green, yellow and red lights.

Partner must have a pretty good hand to splinter opposite a one-level overcall. You have an excellent hand, despite having only four hearts. Your 4♠ is a **green light** bid saying, 'I have a good hand, and first-round spade control'. Instead, 4♡ would have been a **red light** and 'pass' neutral, or a **yellow light**.

Now partner has cuebid the ♣A, and RHO has doubled again. This is not good. Partner is marked with club length, which you are as well. If RHO has good clubs, you likely have at least two club losers. Now 5♡ is a **red light** saying, 'I really don't think we should bid any higher'. If partner trusts you, he will pass unless he was trying for seven.

The full deal:

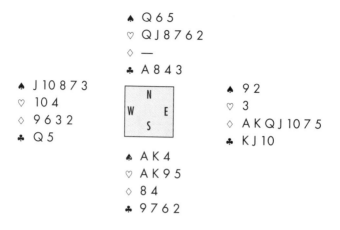

```
                        ♠ Q 6 5
                        ♡ Q J 8 7 6 2
                        ◇ —
                        ♣ A 8 4 3
  ♠ J 10 8 7 3                               ♠ 9 2
  ♡ 10 4            N                         ♡ 3
  ◇ 9 6 3 2      W     E                      ◇ A K Q J 10 7 5
  ♣ Q 5            S                          ♣ K J 10
                        ♠ A K 4
                        ♡ A K 9 5
                        ◇ 8 4
                        ♣ 9 7 6 2
```

SOLUTION 40

Neither vulnerable at IMPs, as South you hold:

♠ J 7 3 ♡ 7 5 4 ◇ 7 4 3 2 ♣ A K 5

WEST	NORTH	EAST	SOUTH
	1♡	pass	2♡¹
3♣	3◇²	pass	?

1. 6-9 pts, 3-card support.
2. Length in diamonds, game try (focus on diamond fit and
   aces and kings in other suits).

The first decision is whether to accept partner's game try. I would say
yes, but barely. I think 3NT is the best call, as it shows where you live
and is the most likely call to benefit partner. Bidding 4♣ is another reasonable possibility. However, I don't like it as much as 3NT since you
have 4-3-3-3 shape; they may be able to get a diamond ruff(s) and the
value of the ♣K is questionable. As it happens, this is exactly what
partner needs to know.

North's hand:

♠ K Q 10 ♡ K Q 10 9 8 ◇ K Q J 10 5 ♣ —

If you bid 4♡, partner will definitely ask for aces, and get your partnership too high.

SOLUTION 41

North-South vulnerable at IMPs, as West you hold:

♠ A Q 9 5 2 ♡ J 2 ◇ A K Q 4 ♣ J 6

WEST	NORTH	EAST	SOUTH
	2♡	pass	3♣
3♠	4◇	4♠	pass
pass	5♣	pass	pass
?			

Again we need to ask ourselves what is going on. North opened in first seat vulnerable with 2♡ and forced his partnership to game in clubs with his 4◇ bid. What does this show?

My guess is diamond control with club support. Looking at your hand, you know it is shortness. Whoops, there goes your defense! It looks as though LHO is either 3-6-1-3 or 2-6-1-4 and has a decent hand. He could even have 3-6-0-4 shape and 6♣ or 7♣ could be cold. Bidding 5♠ is reasonable if you think you can beat 6♣. If you don't, pass!

In the 2006 World Bridge Championships, Branco from Brazil was apparently mesmerized by his diamond honors and doubled 5♣. The full deal:

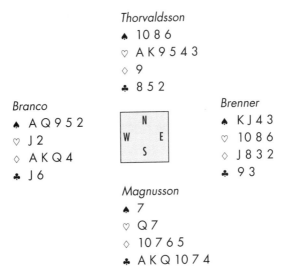

Thorvaldsson
♠ 10 8 6
♡ A K 9 5 4 3
◇ 9
♣ 8 5 2

Branco
♠ A Q 9 5 2
♡ J 2
◇ A K Q 4
♣ J 6

Brenner
♠ K J 4 3
♡ 10 8 6
◇ J 8 3 2
♣ 9 3

Magnusson
♠ 7
♡ Q 7
◇ 10 7 6 5
♣ A K Q 10 7 4

SOLUTION 42

North-South vulnerable at IMPs, as West you hold:

♠ A Q J 10 7 ♡ A K Q 10 2 ◇ A 9 3 ♣ —

WEST	NORTH	EAST	SOUTH
2♣	pass	2◇[1]	pass
2♠	pass	2NT	pass
3♡	pass	3NT	pass
?			

1. Waiting.

Bid 4◇. The only other possibility is 4♡. The main reason that 4◇ is superior is that it caters to partner either having a single-suited diamond hand such as ◇KQ876 or ◇KJ7642, or diamond values with some major-suit fit. Also over 4◇, partner can bid 4♡, to show three of them.

If you bid 4♡, partner doesn't know how to value his diamond or club cards.

Partner held:

♠ 5 ♡ 9 7 3 ◇ K Q J 6 ♣ J 8 6 3 2

Over 4◇ he would have an easy 5♡ bid, which you would raise to 6♡. Iceland's Bjarni Einarsson, in the 2006 Rosenblum Cup, bid 4♡ and played it there.

SOLUTION 43

East-West vulnerable at IMPs, as South you hold:

♠ K 7 6 ♡ 8 ◇ A J 9 5 4 3 ♣ A 10 3

WEST	NORTH	EAST	SOUTH
			1◇
pass	1♡	1♠	2◇
2♠	3◇	3♡	pass
3♠	pass	pass	?

Pass. The 3♡ bid is ominous. It sounds as though partner has only moderate support for your diamonds, and therefore there may be some length on your left. That 3♠ contract does not look cold either.

The full deal:

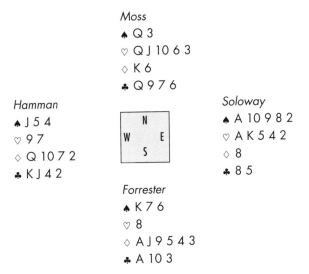

Moss
♠ Q 3
♡ Q J 10 6 3
◇ K 6
♣ Q 9 7 6

Hamman
♠ J 5 4
♡ 9 7
◇ Q 10 7 2
♣ K J 4 2

Soloway
♠ A 10 9 8 2
♡ A K 5 4 2
◇ 8
♣ 8 5

Forrester
♠ K 7 6
♡ 8
◇ A J 9 5 4 3
♣ A 10 3

Forrester bid 4◇, went –50, and lost 6 IMPs in the 2006 Rosenblum Cup when his partners were –200 in 3♠.

SOLUTION 44

Both vulnerable at IMPs, as South you hold:

♠ K 8 6 4 3 ♡ A K Q J ◇ J 5 ♣ 5 2

WEST	NORTH	EAST	SOUTH
			1♠
pass	1NT	2◇	2♡
pass	3♡	4◇	pass
pass	dbl	pass	?

Alan Sontag bid 4♡ in the final of the 2005 Senior Bowl—did you do better?

> *Bridge player: What is it like to*
> *partner a real expert?*
> *Helen Sobel: Why don't you ask Charlie?*
> – Helen Sobel, long-time partner
> of Charles Goren

The full deal:

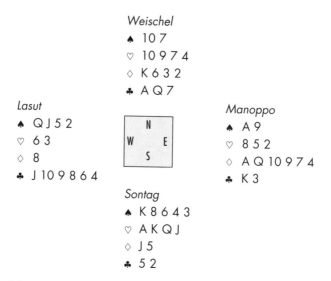

Weischel
♠ 10 7
♡ 10 9 7 4
♢ K 6 3 2
♣ A Q 7

Lasut
♠ Q J 5 2
♡ 6 3
♢ 8
♣ J 10 9 8 6 4

Manoppo
♠ A 9
♡ 8 5 2
♢ A Q 10 9 7 4
♣ K 3

Sontag
♠ K 8 6 4 3
♡ A K Q J
♢ J 5
♣ 5 2

Why would you bid 4♡? Your pass said that you are not accepting the game invite, thus have a minimum. Partner has doubled, which is 90% for penalties. He could have passed trying for a small plus. You have your bid: trust partner and pass.

SOLUTION 45

Neither vulnerable at IMPs, as West you hold:

♠ Q 5 2 ♡ 8 4 3 2 ♢ K 9 ♣ K Q 8 6

WEST	NORTH	EAST	SOUTH
pass	pass	1♣	1♡
dbl	pass	2♡	pass
3♣	pass	3♠	pass
?			

Let's review the auction. Your double was negative, ostensibly promising four spades. Partner bid 2♡, creating a game force. Your 3♣ shows either primary club support with fewer than four spades or some kind of good hand for spades (the implied agreed suit). Partner now bid 3♠, thinking that this set the suit in case slam was in the offing.

You have a very good hand and should be interested in a club slam. The way to tell partner that is to bid 4♣. This should confirm the first type of hand mentioned above, and lead to your reaching the good club slam. Partner held:

♠ A K 9 4 ♡ 9 ◇ A Q J 10 ♣ A 9 4 2

Playing against Sweden in the 2005 Bermuda Bowl, Egypt's Heshmat bid 4♠ and played it there.

SOLUTION 46

East-West vulnerable at IMPs, as East you hold:

♠ A Q 10 9 7 6 ♡ K Q 9 ◇ 5 ♣ Q 8 2

WEST	NORTH	EAST	SOUTH
			1♡
2NT	3♣¹	?	

1. Limit raise in hearts.

This deal swung 17 IMPs to the Hollman team in the 2006 Spingold, capping a remarkable victory, overcoming a 76-IMP half-time deficit. The full deal:

Billy Cohen
♠ K J 8 3
♡ A 5 4 3
◇ 9
♣ 7 6 5 3

♠ 5 2
♡ —
◇ K 8 7 4 3 2
♣ K J 10 9 4

```
      N
   W     E
      S
```

♠ A Q 10 9 7 6
♡ K Q 9
◇ 5
♣ Q 8 2

Ron Smith
♠ 4
♡ J 10 8 7 6 2
◇ A Q J 10 6
♣ A

East doubled 3♣, and doubled Smith's 4♡ bid. Smith redoubled, and made it.

At the other table, this was the auction:

WEST	NORTH	EAST	SOUTH
Grue	Martel	Cheek	Stansby
			1♡
2NT	3♣¹	3♠	4♡
4♠	dbl	all pass	

1. Limit raise in hearts.

Curtis Cheek's 3♠ is a much better bid, as it involves partner in what will likely be a very competitive auction. Four spades doubled made on the nose.

SOLUTION 47

Neither vulnerable at IMPs, as North you hold:

♠ K 7 3 ♡ A 7 6 5 4 2 ◊ K 7 ♣ A 2

WEST	NORTH	EAST	SOUTH
	1♡	pass	2♣
2♠	pass	pass	3◊
pass	?		

There are three choices: 3NT, 3♡ and 4♣. No question 3NT is the gut reaction: no three-card support for partner and a spade stopper. Meanwhile, 3♡ should be your third choice as your suit is so anemic. Playing in the 2006 CNTC, I bid 4♣, which I believe is the best call. I have good trump support, a diamond honor and a ruffing value, the ♡A and a spade control. Partner needs to have this information to make the right decision. Gohl held:

♠ J ♡ — ◊ A Q 6 4 2 ♣ K Q 10 8 7 5 3

Over 4♣ we had an easy time bidding 6♣, gaining 11 IMPs when the opponents played in 5♣ after a less encouraging auction.

SOLUTION 48

Both vulnerable at IMPs, as South you hold:

♠ 10 4 3   ♡ Q   ◊ 8 7 3   ♣ A Q 10 9 4 2

WEST	NORTH	EAST	SOUTH
	1♠	dbl	2♡¹
dbl	2♠	pass	?

1. Constructive spade raise.

There is a good chance that West will bid again, and that will leave your partnership poorly placed to make an informed decision. I bid 3♣ at the table. You may still have a game, and 3♣ describes your hand extremely well. If they do bid more, partner will be able to make the right choice, plus he will know what to lead in case you end up defending.

Partner held

♠ A K J 6 5 2   ♡ 6 5 4   ◊ 9   ♣ K 6 5

and had an easy 4♠ bid. We made five.

SOLUTION 49

North-South vulnerable at IMPs, as North you hold:

♠ A K Q 8 4   ♡ A J 9 6 5   ◊ 8 3   ♣ A

WEST	NORTH	EAST	SOUTH
		pass	1◊
pass	1♠	pass	2◊
pass	2♡	pass	3◊
pass	?		

I asked for aces, looking for a grand in diamonds. Yes, you haven't shown your five hearts yet. Nor have you shown your strength. But partner has shown all you needed to know—he has diamonds, diamonds and more diamonds in a minimum hand. At least seven of them. Unfortunately, we were off a keycard and had to settle for 6◊. Partner's hand (from the 2006 CNTC):

♠ 10   ♡ K 3   ◊ A Q 10 9 7 6 4   ♣ Q 5 4

SOLUTION 50

North-South vulnerable at IMPs, as South you hold:

♠ A K 4 ♡ Q 10 9 8 4 ◊ 8 ♣ 7 5 4 2

WEST	NORTH	EAST	SOUTH
3♠	dbl	pass	4♡
pass	4♠	pass	?

This hand is from *The Bridge World* May 1984 edition of 'Challenge the Champs'. Bidding 5♠ is possible, but I prefer 4NT asking for keycards. Partner is marked with a singleton or void in spades and a huge hand, since you could have very little or even nothing for your forced 4♡ bid. Once partner shows the missing keycards, ask for kings! Don't give up on the grand. Partner should not play you for more, as you only bid 4♡ initially. Neither pair of contestants got to 7♡. The hand opposite:

♠ 6 ♡ A K 6 ◊ A 7 5 3 ♣ A K Q J 9

> *It's not enough to win the tricks*
> *that belong to you. Try also for some*
> *that belong to the opponents.*
> – Alfred Sheinwold

SOLUTION 51

North-South vulnerable at IMPs, as South you hold:

♠ A 10 4 3 ♡ A K 5 ◊ 10 9 3 ♣ Q 9 4

WEST	NORTH	EAST	SOUTH
			1NT[1]
pass	4◊[2]	4♠	?

1. 12-14 HCP.
2. Transfer to hearts.

At the 2006 CNTC, I bid 5♡. In retrospect I think this was wrong, and it was certainly wrong at the table:

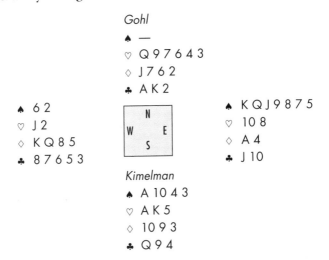

Gohl

♠ —
♡ Q 9 7 6 4 3
♢ J 7 6 2
♣ A K 2

♠ 6 2
♡ J 2
♢ K Q 8 5
♣ 8 7 6 5 3

♠ K Q J 9 8 7 5
♡ 10 8
♢ A 4
♣ J 10

Kimelman

♠ A 10 4 3
♡ A K 5
♢ 10 9 3
♣ Q 9 4

You have two spade tricks on defense but your hearts are good for either playing or defending. The key is that your minor holdings are the worst possible for declaring 5♡.

SOLUTION 52

North-South vulnerable at IMPs, as West you hold:

♠ J 10 6 5 4   ♡ A 10 5   ♢ Q J 5 3   ♣ A

WEST	NORTH	EAST	SOUTH
			1♠
pass	pass	2♡	3♠
?			

This hand caused two large swings in the semifinals of the 1982 Spingold. Before we look at the full deal, let's analyze our holding.

The first thing that leaps out is five spades—the suit our vulnerable RHO bid at the three-level. We also have a good fit in partner's suit, and many other values that should help both the play and defense. However, you should definitely try to declare this hand. RHO will likely have seven spades like ♠AKQ9873, with all the spots we do not have. North-South will also have some tricks outside of spades, likely in diamonds. So South will probably be able to make six spade tricks (ruffing hearts low) and a couple of outside tricks. So bid 4♡. Billy Cohen, in my opinion, showed poor judgment when he doubled 3♠, winding up −730.

In the other semifinal, both Wests bid 4♡, but Reinhold's Pavlicek redoubled when LHO Hamman doubled, and went +880 to win 9 IMPs. The full deal:

```
                    ♠ 2
                    ♡ J 6 4 3
                    ◇ A 9 8 6
                    ♣ 10 6 5 3
♠ J 10 6 5 4                        ♠ 7
♡ A 10 5          ┌─────────┐       ♡ K Q 9 8 7 2
◇ Q J 5 3        │    N    │       ◇ 10 7
♣ A             │ W     E │       ♣ K Q J 7
                 │    S    │
                 └─────────┘
                    ♠ A K Q 9 8 3
                    ♡ —
                    ◇ K 4 2
                    ♣ 9 8 4 2
```

SOLUTION 53

North-South vulnerable at IMPs, as South you hold:

♠ J 7 3 2   ♡ A 9 4   ◇ —   ♣ A K 7 5 4 3

WEST	NORTH	EAST	SOUTH
2♠[1]	pass	3◇	pass
pass	4♠	pass	?

1. A weak preempt in any suit.

This was one of the most discussed hands at the 2005 World Championships.

The full deal:

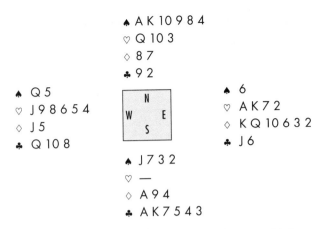

On the actual auction, I would try to get to 7♠, but would force to 6♠. I cannot explain South's pass of 4♠ on the above auction!

There are two interesting facts about this deal. First, at ten tables the bidding went a Multi 2◇ by West, 3◇ by East, all pass! Second, at the other end of the spectrum, there were two pairs that did find 7♠. I am happy to say that Canadians Pierre Daigneault and Stephen Brown were one of them. Pierre and Stephen did it in the Senior Bowl, on the following auction:

WEST	NORTH	EAST	SOUTH
pass	2♠	3◇	4◇
pass	4♡	pass	5NT
pass	6♠[1]	pass	7♠
all pass			

1. Ace and king of trumps; no queen; no extra length.

SOLUTION 54

Both vulnerable at IMPs, as South you hold:

♠ A ♡ K Q ◇ K J 8 5 4 3 ♣ A 10 8 6

WEST	NORTH	EAST	SOUTH
			1◇
pass	1♠	pass	2♣
pass	2♡	pass	3◇
pass	3NT	pass	?

You have done a good job describing your distribution, but not your extra values. You can do this by bidding 4NT. When a trump suit has not been found, a raise of a notrump bid, whether it is 2NT or 3NT, to 4NT is quantitative.

On the actual deal, from the 2005 US Bridge Championships, partner had an easy 6◇ bid holding:

♠ Q J 8 5 4 ♡ A 9 7 4 ◇ Q 2 ♣ K 2

Notice that he bid 3NT and not 4◇ over 3◇, with minimum game-forcing values.

SOLUTION 55

North-South vulnerable at IMPs, as North you hold:

♠ A K 9 3 ♡ Q ◇ A J 8 7 2 ♣ 9 8 2

WEST	NORTH	EAST	SOUTH
	1◇	pass	1♡
pass	1♠	pass	2♣[1]
pass	2◇	pass	2♡
pass	3♣	pass	3◇
pass	?		

1. Fourth suit, game forcing.

Bid 3♡. You have denied three hearts with your nebulous 3♣ bid. Partner has given you one more chance to show heart support.

This hand is from one of the semifinals of the first CNTC event, held in 1980. Mike Chomyn bid 3NT and played it there opposite:

♠ Q 8 4 ♡ A K J 10 8 2 ◇ K 3 ♣ A 4

Keith Balcombe showed much better judgment when he chose to bid 3♡ over 2♡ in the identical auction, and bid and made the excellent grand slam in hearts for a huge pick-up.

SOLUTION 56

North-South vulnerable at IMPs, as West you hold:

♠ 4 2 ♡ A K Q 4 ◇ K 10 7 ♣ Q 9 6 2

WEST	NORTH	EAST	SOUTH
	pass	pass	1♠
dbl	2NT[1]	3♡	3♠
?			

1. Limit raise in spades.

You have a normal takeout double. Partner is competing at the three-level. It looks like you don't have much defense against a spade contract. Pass!

Bart Bramley bid 4♡, South bid 4♠, partner doubled and they made five!

The full deal:

```
              ♠ 9 7 5 3
              ♡ J 10 2
              ◇ A Q 3 2
              ♣ K 8
♠ 4 2                        ♠ A
♡ A K Q 4        N          ♡ 9 8 6 5 3
◇ K 10 7    W        E      ◇ J 8 6 5
♣ Q 9 6 2        S          ♣ J 7 3
              ♠ K Q J 10 8 6
              ♡ 7
              ◇ 9 4
              ♣ A 10 5 4
```

Had Bramley passed, I believe it would have gone 'all pass'.

SOLUTION 57

Neither vulnerable at IMPs, as North you hold:

♠ 9 7 6 4　♡ 3　◇ J 8 2　♣ J 8 7 6 2

WEST	NORTH	EAST	SOUTH
		2♡	dbl
3♣[1]	pass	3♡	3♠
4♡	4♠	pass	pass
5♡	?		

1. Lead-directing.

Double is out as that shows a strong preference for defending. That leaves 5♠ and pass. Given that partner passed 4♠, 5♠ may not make, despite partner having a good hand. Pass, and if partner doubles, pass again.

One key is that the 3♣ bid did not excite East, suggesting he has club shortness. The full deal, from the 2006 Rosenblum Cup final:

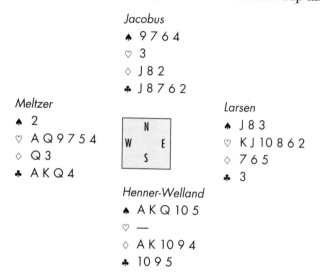

Jacobus
- ♠ 9 7 6 4
- ♡ 3
- ◇ J 8 2
- ♣ J 8 7 6 2

Meltzer
- ♠ 2
- ♡ A Q 9 7 5 4
- ◇ Q 3
- ♣ A K Q 4

Larsen
- ♠ J 8 3
- ♡ K J 10 8 6 2
- ◇ 7 6 5
- ♣ 3

Henner-Welland
- ♠ A K Q 10 5
- ♡ —
- ◇ A K 10 9 4
- ♣ 10 9 5

Marc Jacobus bid 5♠, trading a possible plus for a definite minus. At the other table, a similar auction arrived at the same juncture. Tor Helness passed 5♡, and passed again when his partner, Geir Helgemo, doubled.

SOLUTION 58

Both vulnerable at IMPs, as South you hold:

♠ A 7 6 5 3 ♡ A K 10 9 4 ◇ 3 ♣ K 4

WEST	NORTH	EAST	SOUTH
	1♣	pass	1♠
dbl	2◇	pass	2♡
pass	2NT	pass	3♡
pass	3NT	pass	?

Partner's likely distribution is 1-2-4-6, but could also be 2-2-4-5 or 2-2-3-6. I say that because he didn't bid 3♠ over 3♡, which would be likely with a doubleton spade. He had already denied 3-card support with his 2NT bid. I think the value bid is 6♣. I prefer this slightly aggressive bid as I doubt that 4♣ will help—you have the vast majority of controls, so partner is unlikely to be able to cooperate. Another advantage of bidding six directly is that the opponents don't have a clear picture of what you have, thus whether to lead/defend actively or passively. You have very good values for a club slam, despite being on a 5-2 fit.

This deal is from a recent NABC. Partner held:

♠ K Q ♡ Q 5 ♢ A 10 9 4 ♣ A Q 10 8 3

All potential slams have a play, with 6♡ maybe being the best.

SOLUTION 59

East-West vulnerable at IMPs, as South you hold:

♠ Q 8 2 ♡ K 9 7 3 ♢ Q 2 ♣ 5 4 3 2.

WEST	NORTH	EAST	SOUTH
			pass
pass	1♢	pass	1♡
pass	3♣	pass	3♢
pass	3♡	pass	?

Let's review the bidding. Partner created a game force with 3♣. Your 3♢ is somewhat ambiguous, and can be later interpreted as encouraging. (At the other table in a 1982 Rosenblum match, Lebel for France bid 3NT instead, which I think is the right call.) If your hearts were a little better, 4♡ would probably be right—still could be. But now 3NT looks wrong and clubs looks right.

Bid 5♣. Partner should get the message and pass. His hand was:

♠ 10 ♡ A Q 10 ♢ A K J 5 4 ♣ A Q 8 6

At the table, Spain's Agero-Diaz compounded his problems by bidding 4♣ and raising 4♢ to 5♢. His partner, Garcia-Viedma, justifiably assumed that 4♣ showed a control and bid 6♢, which had two sure losers.

SOLUTION 60

Both vulnerable at IMPs, as South you hold:

♠ A 4 ♡ A K Q 8 5 ◇ — ♣ A K 10 4 3 2

WEST	NORTH	EAST	SOUTH
			?

What is your call?

This hand is from the 1982 Spingold semifinal. Billy Cohen opened 1♣ and heard partner Mark Molson bid 1♡ on:

♠ K 9 5 3 ♡ 7 6 4 3 2 ◇ 7 ♣ 8 7 5

His next bid was 7♡! Fortunately, he picked up the clubs.

At the other table, Goldman reasonably opened 2♣, but strong interference prevented him and his partner Soloway from bidding 7♡. The lesson from this hand is not whether to bid 6♡ or 7♡, but to consider opening strong distributional hands at the one-level. This helps to elicit more information not only from partner but also from the opponents, useful when coping with strong interference, as they will likely be distributional as well.

> *The dog too old to learn new tricks*
> *always has been.*
> - Anonymous

SOLUTION 61

Both vulnerable at IMPs, as South you hold:

♠ K 4 ♡ A Q 7 ◇ J 8 7 4 2 ♣ K Q 10

WEST	NORTH	EAST	SOUTH
1♣	pass	1♡	?

Pass! Yes, you have a good hand, but you have only one of the unbid suits, and partner has a maximum of 7 HCP. Thus, you do not have a game. The full deal:

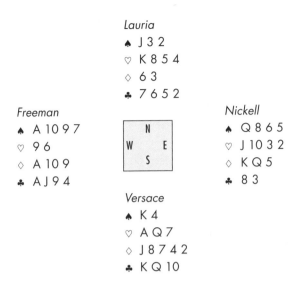

Lauria
♠ J 3 2
♡ K 8 5 4
◇ 6 3
♣ 7 6 5 2

Freeman
♠ A 10 9 7
♡ 9 6
◇ A 10 9
♣ A J 9 4

Nickell
♠ Q 8 6 5
♡ J 10 3 2
◇ K Q 5
♣ 8 3

Versace
♠ K 4
♡ A Q 7
◇ J 8 7 4 2
♣ K Q 10

In the 2005 Bermuda Bowl final, Italy vs. USA, Versace bid 1NT and, in my view, deservedly got doubled, went for –500 and lost 9 IMPs.

SOLUTION 62

East-West vulnerable at IMPs, as South you hold:

♠ — ♡ Q J 10 ◇ A 10 8 7 6 5 ♣ K 8 6 4

WEST	NORTH	EAST	SOUTH
1♠	pass	pass	dbl
2♡	dbl	3♠	pass
pass	dbl	pass	?

Trust partner and pass. What's going on? Partner has a trap pass of 1♠, and his double of 2♡ is alerting you to this fact. You may ask, why can't partner just have hearts with values? Since South just balanced, any strong action by North shows at least an opening bid with unsuitable shape for any type of initial action. This implies spade length. If partner had an opening bid with a spade stopper, then 2NT or quite possibly 3NT would be a good value bid over 2♡. If North instead had, let's say, 10 points and hearts, he would just pass. The problem with North just passing 2♡ with a trap pass of spades is that it could well go 'all pass', because South would have no clue about partner's hand.

Partner actually held

♠ K J 10 9 ♡ A 8 7 ◇ Q 2 ♣ A 10 7 5

and three spades doubled was down three, to give us +800 at a recent tournament.

SOLUTION 63

Neither vulnerable at IMPs, as West you hold:

♠ A K 10 ♡ 10 8 7 ◇ A K J 8 7 4 ♣ 7

WEST	NORTH	EAST	SOUTH
1◇	4♡	5◇	pass
?			

There is no right or wrong answer for this hand. I will show you partner's hand very shortly.

Despite there being no guarantees, I would bid 6◇. Yes, we might be off two heart tricks. But what does partner have to commit our side to the five-level? Certainly not great diamonds. In fact, I might hold no more than three diamonds for my opener. I certainly don't have to have the ♠A or ♠K—maybe I have good clubs.

I think if he can bid five, you can bid six. Eddie Kantar passed and lost 11 IMPs when Kokish and Nagy got to six on a different auction. Partner held:

♠ Q J 5 4 ♡ A ◇ Q 10 5 2 ♣ K 9 8 3

About the Author

Neil Kimelman is 53 years old and lives in Winnipeg, Manitoba. He has been playing bridge since he was nine years old.

Despite taking a fifteen-year sabbatical to focus on his career and family, he has placed in the top ten in many of the relatively few NABC and CNTC events that he has played in over the years. These include the Reisinger (twice), NABC Open Pairs (twice), Life Master Pairs, COPC pairs (six times) and CNTC (ten times). He has over fifty regional wins to his credit.

He is married to Colleen, his wife of 27 years, and has two children—Erin, 25, and Kyle, 21.

He plans on playing much more bridge after he retires later in 2008.

Marquis Book Printing Inc.

Québec, Canada
2008